Politics
on the Margins

Politics
on the Margins

Restructuring and the
Canadian Women's Movement

Janine Brodie

Fernwood Publishing
Halifax

Editing: Anne Webb
Design and layout: Beverley Rach
Cover Photos: Janine Brodie
Printed and bound in Canada by: Hignell Printing Limited

A publication of:
Fernwood Publishing
Box 9409, Station A
Halifax, Nova Scotia
B3K 5S3

Fernwood Publishing Company Limited gratefully acknowledges the financial support of The Ministry of Canadian Heritage.

Canadian Cataloguing in Publication Data
Brodie, M. Janine, 1952-
Politics on the margins

(Basics from Fernwood Publishing)

Includes bibliographical references.
ISBN 1-895686-47-4

1. Feminism -- Canada. 2. State, The. I. Title.

HQ1236.5.C3B76 1995   305.42'0971   C95-950063-4

CONTENTS

For my mother
Jean Margaret Noble Brodie

PREFACE

THIS BOOK IS THE OUTCOME OF TWO years of thinking and talking about the implications of the current era of restructuring and the emergence of the neoliberal state for Canadian women, the women's movement, and new social movements more generally. I wish to thank my good friend and colleague Isabella Bakker for initially encouraging me to explore this question and for faithfully reading my many attempts to grapple with it. And many attempts there have been! During my tenure as the Robarts Chair in Canadian Studies at York University in 1994-95, I wrote several conference papers touching on various aspects of this topic. It was also the focus of the Robarts Annual Lecture. I am grateful to both the Robarts Centre and to the Social Sciences and Humanities Research Council for their support of this project. I would also like to thank Errol Sharpe of Fernwood Publishing for patiently waiting for this final product and Anne Webb for her skilled editing.

The current restructuring process is far from complete and its impacts on social programs and social movements are still unfolding. Writing about it, then, is very much like taking aim at a moving target. A number of people have helped me sharpen my focus, although, I am sure, it is not yet sharp enough. Among them are members of the SSHRC strategic Women and Restructuring network—Isabella Bakker (principal), Majorie Cohen, Pat Connelly, Carla Lipsig-Mumme, Meg Luxton, and Martha MacDonald; the past and present Directors of the Robarts Centre for Canadian Studies—Kenneth McRoberts and Daniel Drache; Caroline Andrew; Jane Arscott; Davina Bhandar; Elaine Cairns; Barbara Cameron; Shelagh Day; Judy Fudge; Chris Gabriel; Stephen Gill; Laurie Gillies; Lise Gotell; Shireen Hassim; Catherine Kellog; Steve Patten; Judy Rebick; Annis May Timpson; Leah Vosko; and Reg Whitaker. Thanks is due as well to my dear friend and "covergirl" Susan O'Rourke. Most of all I owe a big debt to Lise, Brodie, and Liam for putting up with my absences and preoccupations.

CHAPTER ONE

The Politics of Uncertainty

ONLY A YEAR AFTER IT HAD TROUNCED the Mulroney Conservatives at the polls, the federal Liberal government announced a series of initiatives which dashed all hopes that it had understood the 1993 vote as a mandate for change. After enduring the severest recession since the 1930s, a twenty-year decline in real incomes, and a decade of Tory cuts to the postwar social welfare system, Minister of Finance Paul Martin told Canadians that they had it "too easy for too long." Launching a discussion paper to guide consultations prior to the 1995 budget, he told us quite simply that we were "in hock up to our eyeballs" and that his commitment to reduce the deficit was "absolute and unequivocal" (*The Toronto Star* 18 October 1994, A1).

At the same time, federal Minister of Human Resources Development Lloyd Axworthy was unveiling his long-awaited discussion paper on redesigning the social welfare system. The minister said the motivation behind the proposed reform of Canada's $39 billion social safety net was to end the "dependency" on some form of social assistance exhibited by 20 percent of the workforce, and to get people back to work (*The Toronto Star* 18 October 1994, A17). A week later a lonely group of anti-poverty activists mounted a demonstration protesting the neoliberal course that the Chretien government was charting for Canada's future. However, their chant—"Jean Chretien shame on you. Your little red book turned Tory blue" —failed to arouse much public attention.

These days Canadians are being bombarded at every turn with the message that things have to change, that we are uncompetitive in an increasingly competitive global economy, and that we can no longer afford the security and services that were once guaranteed to all Canadians by the postwar welfare state. The past decade has ushered in a period of complex

9

change which is far more encompassing and transformative than perhaps many of us have yet to fully appreciate. Canada, as our politicians seem fond of reminding us, is currently mired in a painful period of "restructuring"— a period of change as fundamental to our political development as the creation of the Keynesian welfare state or, indeed, of Confederation itself. And, contrary to the rhetoric of Bay Street analysts, this restructuring has not been limited to the markets or to the so-called "imperatives" of the new global economy. Instead, we are embedded in a process of renegotiating basic political conventions and cultural forms, among them our shared "common sense" understandings of the appropriate boundaries between the international and the national, the state and the economy, the public and the domestic spheres, and the very definition of what it means to be a citizen.

This book examines how the politics of restructuring has eroded many of the common sense understandings of politics that Canadians have shared for the past fifty years, and how these changes have challenged the survival of the Canadian women's movement. I argue that the disappearance of the Keynesian welfare state and the radical redrawing of the boundaries between the public sphere, the market, and the home are eroding the very political identities and public spaces that empowered postwar Canadian feminism and distinguished it from its turn-of-the-century counterpart.

For the past twenty-five years, Canada has witnessed the unprecedented growth in size and influence of what is commonly termed the "second wave" of the Canadian women's movement. Since its meagre presence in the late 1960s as a small but influential group of urban, white, middle-class women, the women's movement has become an important coalition of Aboriginal women, women of colour, labour feminists, lesbians, professional women, women with disabilities, poor women, and other activists. It is also one of the clearest voices for social, political and economic justice in Canadian politics (Khosla 1993, 1). The current era of restructuring, however, presents a challenge to the women's movement because it is altering in fundamental ways the state, gender relations, and the objectives of political struggle. Despite some victories, the "goal of equality for women is, in real terms, facing the most concrete and profound backlash of the post World War II period" (ibid).

It is now widely acknowledged that the women's movement has been radically challenged by the ascendency of neoliberalism as the new wisdom of governing. Increasingly, feminists are becoming disillusioned with how little they have achieved in the past twenty years and how quickly these gains have been eroded (Chapman 1993, 195). Recently, Judy Rebick, past president of the National Action Committee on the Status of Women (NAC), described the major challenges that the current era poses for the Canadian women's movement. First, she argues that the current preoccupation in

Canadian politics with the deficit has had the effect of completely marginalizing women's issues because "most concerns of women either require government expenditure or intervention and both are really out of fashion right now." Second, she observes that it is very difficult to insert considerations of gender equality into current political debates about economic restructuring because "when you talk about women's issues immediately it is more narrowly defined" to mean abortion, pay equity and other specific concerns. Third, Rebick argues that many women's organizations may not survive cuts in government funding. And, finally, she predicts that the backlash that the women's movement confronted in the late 1980s is likely to intensify in the 1990s and beyond. As a result, Rebick suggests "we're going to be back to a situation much like the '60s where the only way to get attention is through grassroots organizing" (1994, 57-61).

What are we to make of these rather pessimistic predictions about the future of the women's movement in Canada? In the chapters which follow I argue that popular feminist theorizing about the interrelationships among women as political actors, the politics of the women's movement, and historical state forms has not grasped the full range of implications of the current era of restructuring. I explore restructuring as the emergence of a new cultural and political form. The politics of restructuring revolve around a multi-faceted contraction and re-regulation of the public and the political realms, as they were constituted by the postwar welfare state, and the simultaneous expansion of the private whether defined as markets or the domestic sphere. This shifting political terrain, in turn, invites the women's movement to engage in new strategic thinking about the very meaning of the public and about the political goals of a potential "third wave" of Canadian feminism.

This chapter provides an overview of the process of restructuring and the emergence of a neoliberal governing philosophy in Canada which celebrates the ideas of market-driven development and free enterprise. In Chapter 2 I examine feminist theories of the state and make the case for viewing the state as an historical and cultural form. In Chapter 3 I review how different state forms have shaped the first and second waves of Canadian feminism. Chapter 4 outlines the key threads of the emerging new political order and state form while Chapter 5 describes how these factors are marginalizing the women's movement in Canadian politics. The concluding chapter also outlines some possible dimensions of a new feminist politics of restructuring.

11

THE 1993 WATERSHED

We need a new architecture—for government,
for the economy. (Paul Martin, Canada 1994a)

The 1993 federal election reflected the sentiment that was becoming increasingly prevalent since the implementation of the Canada-US Free Trade Agreement (CUFTA) in 1989. Canadian voters dealt a deathblow to the federal Conservative party for betraying their "sacred trusts," dismantling their cultural icons, eroding the welfare state, and forcing their family members into the growing ranks of the unemployed—all in the name of "efficiency" and "competitiveness." But, the force behind this collective rage was not a drive to restore the postwar welfare state that the Conservatives had dismantled with such determination and assuredness since their election in 1984. Although public opinion polls show that most Canadians continue to support their social programs, the only party promising anything like a return to the "good old" Keynesian days, the federal New Democratic Party (NDP), was dismissed during the campaign as the "New Preservation Party," and abandoned at the polls by all but its most loyal supporters.

Perhaps not since the 1935 election, which also was held during a prolonged period of economic turmoil and political uncertainty, had voters been offered such distinct choices between the federal parties, their respective understandings of Canada's economic and political crises, and their visions for the future. For most of the postwar period, Canada's three major parties shared similar assumptions about the appropriate relationship between the state, the economy, and the home. These shared assumptions, sometimes called the "Keynesian" or "postwar" consensus, rested on three fundamental planks:

- the development of a comprehensive social welfare system,
- the use of macroeconomic levers (taxation and money supply) to control inflation or stimulate growth and to protect the national economy from international disturbances,
- adherence to a more liberalized international trading regime (Brodie 1990, 149).

The three major parties were committed to these principles, arguing only about how much welfare or how much government intervention in the economy was appropriate. Other federal parties which did not completely buy into the postwar consensus, such as the Creditistes of the 1960s, which relied on Social Credit doctrine, were marginalized in political debates and managed to persuade only temporary converts in the electorate (Brodie and

Jenson 1988). The postwar consensus changed our common sense notions of the government-market relation and, indeed, what it meant to be a Canadian. Contrary to current political discourse, it was widely believed that there was no such thing as a self-regulating market. Political control of the economy was "almost a moral imperative" (McBride and Shields 1993, 10). Canadian citizenship came to mean more than having formal rights such as the right to vote or join a union. Instead, the menu of citizen rights came to include social welfare claims which everyone could make simply because they were Canadians (ibid., 15).

On these issues almost everyone agreed. In fact, so embracing was this consensus in the postwar party system that it was often hard for voters to discern any tangible or lasting differences between the two major federal parties. Political commentators often referred to the federal Liberal and Conservative Parties as "Tweedledum and Tweedledee" or "The Boys From Bay Street." Meanwhile, the "different" party, the social democratic New Democratic Party, was dismissed as little more than "Liberals in a hurry!"

In the mid-1970s, this consensus began to break down. Since that time, the prolonged economic crisis and the rise of neoliberal governing practices have dramatically changed the political landscape in which policy-makers assess both the causes of and "cures" for Canada's ongoing social problems. By 1993, it became clear that the neoliberalism of the Mulroney years was neither a partisan matter nor an historical aberration. Canadian voters gave a resounding majority to the federal Liberal Party which promised little more than to be a more compassionate manager of the economic transition than its more overtly neoliberal predecessors. And, it is now flanked in the House of Commons by new players—the Bloc Quebecois which is dedicated to the dissolution of Canada, and the Reform Party which would completely dismantle the welfare state. The federal party system has been transformed, now housing new challengers with profoundly different prescriptions for Canadian development, nationhood, and citizenship. The postwar pattern of politics, in other words, has been pushed aside, revealing in stark relief the uncertain and contested political space we are now occupying (Brodie and Jenson 1995).

The 1993 federal election marked a profound change in the text of federal politics as well as in its many subtexts, including the issue of gender equality and the influence of the women's movement. The press heralded the election as a breakthrough for women in Canadian politics because two of the major party leaders were women. News coverage brimmed with stories speculating about different male and female leadership styles. We learned, for example, that NDP leader Audrey MacLaughlin washes her own dishes and that Progressive Conservative leader, Kim Campbell, has square-dancing prowess. At the same time, however, the federal parties were virtually silent about so-called women's issues. In fact, the two major parties obviously felt that gender was so irrelevant that they could refuse to debate women's issues—something they had done in the two previous federal campaigns—without paying significant electoral penalties.

Yet, all of this passed with little commentary. Few seemed to notice that the mere presence of female bodies in the federal election was being used by the major parties and the press as a proxy for talking about women's issues—especially about how the demise of the welfare state and the restructuring of the Canadian economy were adversely affecting the everyday lives of Canadian women. In the process, feminist organizations concerned with the substance of women's lives were written out of the election script. It is precisely the goal of this book to demonstrate how the new governing order is systematically writing women and the women's movement out of the Canadian political debate.

THE DECLINE OF THE POSTWAR ORDER

Canada, like all western democracies, is currently experiencing a profound shift in state form and governing practices. It is now widely acknowledged that the foundations of the Keynesian welfare state (KWS) have not survived the combined forces of prolonged recession, jobless growth, the so-called globalization of production, and neoliberal governing practices. The broad consensus that grounded the KWS and structured the pattern of federal politics for almost a half century has gradually, but certainly, given way to a very different set of assumptions about the role of government and the rights of citizens. These new assumptions and understandings both structure new forms of domination and, at the same time, reshape more familiar ones rooted in gender, race, and class.

Canada is not the only country to be submerged in a politics of disruption, uncertainty, and change. In Britain, for example, the left has termed this period of change as the "New Times." Since the early 1980s, most western liberal democracies have been forced to re-examine many of their governing assumptions and practices, moving from what some political economists have called a Fordist past to an unknown Post-Fordist future. According to the regulation theorists, the economies and politics of western democracies were organized around what is termed a Fordist "mode of regulation." By this they mean that for much of the post-World War II period there was a widespread consensus that national governments should take an active role in managing the economy through Keynesian demand management techniques; the labour process was organized around the assembly line; and redistribution was accomplished through social welfare spending and collective bargaining (Lipietz 1987).

Unlike the previous doctrine of the laissez-faire state which governed the western world until the Great Depression of the 1930s, the postwar years brought new shared understandings about state intervention in the economy, an elaboration of bureaucratic institutions and governing instruments, and an expansion of the very meaning of citizenship itself. The Keynesian state asserted the primacy of the state over the "invisible hand" of the market and engendered widespread public expectations that governments were responsible for meeting the basic needs of their citizens. Fordism, then, was a whole package of relations, institutions, and arrangements which linked a logic of economic development during a particular historical period (the regime of accumulation, i.e., mass consumption) with an equally particular and complementary set of norms, habits, laws, regulations, and representations of reality (the mode of regulation, i.e., among many other things, the welfare state) (Harvey 1989, 121-23).

Although the regulation theorists are decidedly silent about gender, Fordism also rested on a very particular model of the workplace, the home, and the gender order. It presumed a stable working and middle class, a nuclear family supported by a male breadwinner, a family wage, a dependent wife and children, and women's unpaid domestic labour. Moreover, this particular organization of cultural forms and gender relations was supported and reinforced by the Keynesian welfare state (McDowell 1991, 400-02).

> We missed the signals that times were changing.
> (Paul Martin, *The Toronto Star* 18 October 1994,
> A1)

The passing of Fordism and the welfare state represents much more than a series of state responses to the changing international economy or to the so-called "debt crisis." It signals a new way of thinking about governing practices—an historic alteration in state form which enacts simultaneous changes in cultural assumptions, political identities, and the very terrain of political struggle. Restructuring is a key word which refers to a prolonged and conflict-ridden political process during which old assumptions and shared understandings are challenged and are eventually either rejected or transformed while social forces struggle to achieve a new consensus—a new vision of the future to fill the vacuum created by the erosion of the old. The concept of restructuring represents the simultaneous "combination of falling apart and building up again" of an entire political-cultural order. As Soja explains, the term conveys "the notion of a 'brake,' if not a break, in secular trends, and a shift toward a significantly different order and configuration of social, economic and political life (1989, 159).

THE NEW LIBERAL ORTHODOXY

Glimpses of the politics of post-Fordism first appeared with the election of Margaret Thatcher's Conservatives in Britain in 1979 and Ronald Reagan's Republicans in the United States in 1980. These two neoliberal leaders were largely successful in changing "the balance between state and society," and creating new coalitions of voters and interests and new common sense understandings of politics (Gamble 1988, 2). Since then, this new governing orthodoxy—the neoliberal consensus—has been crafted. It now tops the political agendas of most western democracies. It holds that changing international realities put roughly the same demands on all governments. They must

- maximize exports
- reduce social spending
- curtail state economic regulation
- enable market forces to restructure national economies as parts of transnational or regional trading blocs (Friedman 1991, 35).

Grounded by these principles, Canadian governments are increasingly rejecting their former postwar roles of promoting domestic welfare and protecting the national economy from unstable international forces. They also have largely abandoned as futile the postwar goals of full employment and an inclusive social safety net. As Liberal Finance Minister Paul Martin summarized in his first budget speech in 1994, "for years, governments have been promising more than they can deliver, and delivering more than they can afford. That has to end. We are ending it" (Canada 1994a, 2).

Seduced by the transparent logic of neoliberalism and nudged by the threats of powerful transnational corporations and international lending agencies, Canadian governments are now effectively acting as the midwives of globalization, transforming state apparatuses, development strategies, and regulations to respond to the "perceived exigencies" of globalization (Cox 1991, 337). We have replaced assumptions and governing practices premised on the notion that there has to be a collective responsibility for individuals. Instead, we are told that government and citizens have to be reformed to achieve the illusive and abstract states of "flexibility" and "competitiveness."

> There are clearly things wrong with our system. It is not operating as it should be operating. . . . Part of what is happening is that the textbook is wrong. Or the textbook doesn't fit the country we've become. (Joe Clarke quoted in Valpy 1993, 181)

Neoliberalism was put at the top of the Canadian political agenda by the Macdonald Commission (The Royal Commission on the Economic Union and Development Prospects for Canada) which released its long-awaited report in 1985. It successfully advanced the position that free trade with the United States and a neoliberal economic agenda were the *only* viable economic development strategies left to Canada. With respect to free trade, in particular, Canadians were told to close their eyes and take "a leap of faith" because the globalization train had already left the station. If Canadians did not "jump aboard," they would most surely be left behind and have to forfeit their living standards. Consequently, the report advised all Canadian governments, federal and provincial, to

- adopt a market-driven development strategy,
- facilitate adjustment by reducing regulations on industry,
- create new opportunities for private sector growth (Brodie 1990, 218-23).

The Macdonald Commission had been appointed in 1982 by the Trudeau administration which, at the time, seemed incapable of reversing Canada's worst economic downturn since the 1930s. Postwar macroeconomic policies seemed unable to cope with stagflation—a simultaneous increase in both inflation and joblessness. The Liberals fell to electoral defeat in 1984. But, the newly elected Conservative government, under the leadership of Brian Mulroney, was quick to embrace the Commission's prescriptions for economic renewal. In fact, the outgoing Liberal government could not have given a better gift to this business elite which was already convinced of the sagacity of neoliberalism. It quickly launched into free trade talks with the United States, although only two years before all but one of the Conservative leadership candidates (John Crosby), including Brian Mulroney, had roundly rejected the idea as a threat to Canadian jobs and sovereignty. The Conservative Party also began, tentatively at first, to carve away at the welfare state.

An uncompromising neoliberal worldview came to dominate the Mulroney government's front benches after its re-election in 1988 and the implementation of the Canada-US Free Trade Agreement in 1989. Throughout the late 1980s, the Mulroney government had used mounting federal deficits as a rationale for cutting back on the welfare state. By the early 1990s, however, the Conservatives' attack was directly linked to making Canada more "competitive." According to their analysis, competitiveness could be realized primarily by forfeiting the economic terrain to the private sector. In its 1992 Budget Speech, for example, the Conservative government announced that its primary legislative priority was to promote greater "reliance on the private sector and market forces" (Abele 1992, 1). Ranked immediately below this were the related goals of deficit reduction, inflation control, free trade, and developing a new consensus about the role of government. For the federal Conservatives, a restructured economy required a restructured government that would provide only those public services that were affordable and did not interfere with Canadian competitiveness in the new global order (McQuaig 1992). Indeed, so committed was the ruling party to this new worldview that it attempted to constitutionalize it in the early stages of the ill-fated Charlottetown Accord negotiations.

MORE OF THE SAME

> The days of government simply nibbling at the edges are over. The practice of endless process with product are gone. Our task is to end the drift. (Paul Martin, Budget Speech, February 1994, 7)

Historians may very well judge the Mulroney regime as one of the most radical and overtly doctrinaire in Canadian history. The Progressive Conservatives ultimately met on a collision course with the Canadian voters in 1993 when the latter gave a landslide victory to the federal Liberal Party. Since the election, however, the new government has charted the same neoliberal course and has used similar governing instruments, primarily the budget, to erode Canada's social safety net. The Liberal government, for example, ratified the North American Free Trade Agreement (NAFTA) in January 1994 even though it had failed to negotiate the side agreements which it had promised, during the election campaign, were "bottom line" requirements which had to be met for Canada to enter the agreement. And, it is now actively encouraging other countries such as Chile to come aboard if they can meet the minimum standards. The Liberals have also prioritized deficit reduction over employment and infrastructure development, and have continued to attack the social welfare programs and system of federal-provincial cost-sharing that was built up piecemeal in the postwar years.

Minister of Finance Paul Martin Jr. wore workboots instead of Bay Street brogues when he delivered his first budget on 22 February 1994. This change in customary footwear was meant to convey the message to voters that the Liberal Party was about jobs and change. It did not signal that the new federal government was preparing to repair Canada's fraying social safety net. Instead, Martin told Parliament that things were going to change. He was preparing to set in motion "the most comprehensive reform of government policy in decades" (Budget Speech, February 1994, 2). In the process, the federal government has continued to totally redesign the social welfare system—an initiative which began within the federal bureaucracy during the Mulroney years. The postwar Keynesian welfare state, in other words, is no more.

CHAPTER TWO

Restructuring, Women and the State

FEMINISTS HAVE NOT STARED PASSIVELY into the face of the emerging new order. Women's organizations in English Canada have been in the forefront of the "popular sector"—a loose coalition of labour, church, anti-poverty, farmer, and Native groups which have been opposed to neoliberal premises and governing practices ever since they were planted on Canadian soil in the early 1980s (Cameron 1989). Feminists also have been among the few to emphasize that restructuring is neither a gender-neutral trading deal nor an economic imperative. Instead, they consistently point out that restructuring is a decidedly gendered process (Bakker 1994).

There is a growing body of gender sensitive research which provides compelling evidence of the pronounced and multiple gendered impacts of restructuring. To date, most of the empirical data on the gendered dimensions of restructuring has come from developing countries where the effects of structural adjustment policies (SAP) were first felt most severely. These policies, which characteristically entail reducing the public sector and reorienting national economies to external trade, have tended to impact on women in five fundamental ways. A recent study conducted for the US Agency for International Development (USAID), for example, shows that everywhere poverty is increasingly gendered. The so-called "feminization of poverty" is particularly acute among female-headed households and among elderly women. Second, women have acted as "shock-absorbers" during adjustment, both by curtailing their own consumption and by increasing their work load to compensate for household income loss. Third, women tend to be more directly affected by reductions in social welfare spending and public programs. Privatization and welfare cuts often simply mean that social services are shifted from the paid work of women in the public sector to the unpaid labour of women in the domestic sphere. Fourth, gains made toward the goal of gender equality during the 1970s are being rapidly eroded due to shifts in the labour market which are producing few good jobs for women (or men, for that matter), and because of reductions in childcare, education, and retraining programs. Finally, public expenditure constraints have a direct impact on women's employment and working conditions within the public sector itself (USAID 1992, xiv). Progress toward employment and pay equity, for example, has come to a standstill.

Canada awaits a comprehensive assessment of the gendered impacts of restructuring. In fact, within most Western countries trade unions and policy-makers have tended to focus on restructuring in the manufacturing sector and, by extension, its impact on men who disproportionately filled the ranks of the unionized manufacturing sector in the postwar years. Nonetheless, feminist academics and women's organizations have begun to paint a grim picture of the gendered underpinnings of the new order. According to a report released by the NAC in 1992, the most general tendencies are among the following:

- Social and economic policies are forcing women to work more for less pay.
- Family incomes are dropping while both the number of hours needed to support a household (45 hours a week in 1970 compared to 65-80 in 1991) and the number of female-headed single parent families have increased dramatically (NAC 1992, 3).
- The number of women working in full-time jobs is shrinking while more have been forced into "flexible" part-time work which is short-term, low paying, and non-unionized or piecework.
- The majority of women working full-time earn less than $20,000 a year.
- The wage gap between women and men remains significant, especially for older women and women with little education. The wage gap between women and men in the thirty-five to forty-four age category is 60 percent.
- Poverty rates among single mothers are at record levels—fully 62% of single mothers live below the poverty line and make on average $2834 less than they did two years ago (Khosla 1993, 1-11, 26).
- Some 70% of Canada's children who depend on public assistance live in single parent families (ECE 1994, 7).
- Restructuring has increased racial and class inequalities among Canadian women themselves.

READING THE RESTRUCTURING PROCESS

Key front-line women's organizations recognized, from the early 1980s, that the neoliberals' vision of a minimalist state and unfettered market-driven development threatened the very foundations of second wave feminism's equity agenda. Throughout the 1960s and 1970s the dominant current of the English Canadian women's movement consistently linked the achievement of gender equality with federal state activism, whether through the elaboration of the social safety net, the regulation of the private sector or law reform (Brodie 1994). Critical policy demands made by feminists, such as for universal and affordable childcare, income security, the protection of women from male violence, affirmative action, and pay equity, all call for more not less governmental intervention and public spending (Gotell and Brodie 1991, 62). It is hardly surprising then that, after the election of the federal Progressive Conservative Party in 1984 and its embrace of free trade in 1985, women's organizations expended ever increasing quantities of their political currency defending the welfare state from the neoliberal onslaught.

Nevertheless, whether in the form of statistical data demonstrating the gendered foundations of restructuring or in the form of political protest, we sometimes fail to give the present era of restructuring an adequate conceptual and strategic reading. Feminists have tended to focus on, as Soja puts it, "the falling apart" without exploring how "the building up again" is proceeding unabated, often in the most subtle and seemingly innocent ways (Soja 1989, 159). This inadequate reading of restructuring, I believe, usually takes one of three forms.

- Liberal Empiricism: The fundamental assumption informing this perspective is that state officials will adopt policy reforms aimed at correcting the gendered impacts of restructuring if they are provided with "good" gender sensitive research.
- Radical Determinism: This approach recognizes the gendered impacts of restructuring but argues that this simply provides additional evidence of the perpetual and fundamental opposition between either the interests of capital and women or of women and men (Yeatman 1990, 119; McDowell 1991, 401).
- Nostalgic Welfarism: This approach valorizes the postwar welfare state and reads any deviation from past experience as undesirable, discounting the fact that this same welfare state also had negative consequences for women and other disadvantaged groups.

These feminist readings of restructuring are inadequate on a number of counts. Liberal empiricism, for example, conveys the questionable assumption that unequal gender impacts are accidental rather than integral to the current

21

round of restructuring. It also places the state outside the restructuring process and assumes that the state can neutralize the gendered effects of the process with the appropriate "facts" and political pressure. It does not explore how shifts in state form are part and parcel of the restructuring process. The second reading, radical determinism, in contrast, sees little hope for change because it envisions the state as always reinforcing, supporting, or acting on behalf of a unity of interests, e.g., capital or men, which lie outside of the state system (Watson 1990). It casts all women at all times and places as passive victims of a state which acts in the interests of the oppressor. At the same time, it fails to recognize that not all women are disadvantaged by restructuring, at least not to the same degree, and that the effects of restructuring can be quite different across racial and class groupings.

Before stating my objections to the third approach, I want to stress that my criticism does not relate to the necessity and moral imperative of the collective provision of social security for all citizens—women, men, and children. I am among those who reject the neoliberal claim that Canadians have no choice but to adjust to the leaner and meaner state that is currently being fashioned in Ottawa through a barrage of neoliberal rhetoric, regulations, and public policies. My point is simply that the postwar welfare state was only one particular kind of state and one particular way to provide social welfare and redistribute income. The postwar welfare state arose out of very different historical circumstances than we face now and was fashioned by different political actors with different political interests, alliances, and motivations. A nostalgic welfarism reading of restructuring puts feminists in the paradoxical position of having to defend the same welfare state that they had previously, and with good reason, criticized for being an agent of social control and for being patriarchal, classist, and racist (Abbott and Wallace 1992, 22). It is also the same welfare state that the neoliberals, over the past decade, have successfully named as responsible for the economic and debt crises.

> We can't return to the aesthetic practices elaborated on the basis of historical situations and dilemmas which are no longer ours. (Jameson 1993, 87)

As the postwar welfare state fades into history it is important to recognize that it was not the endpoint in the history of state formation—the end of politics—for women or anyone else. Instead, it was a rather short-lived, precarious, and geographically isolated manifestation of political organization and state form. In the next section of this chapter I argue that a feminist reading of the restructuring process must begin with the premise that this process simultaneously alters the economic, public, and the domestic; the very constitution of gendered political actors; and, ultimately, the objects of feminist political struggle.

FEMINIST THEORIZING ABOUT THE STATE

Feminist theorizing about the state has followed several different paths, all of which, some would argue, have ended in a conceptual deadend. Liberal feminists, for example, have been criticized for their optimistic depiction of the liberal democratic state as a potentially progressive and sovereign institution which, once "purged" of its sexism, is capable of legislating women's equality (Watson 1990, 7). For such critics, public policy and law are incapable of realizing women's equality unless they are accompanied by a fundamental reorganization of society, including the public and private spheres and gender roles.

At the same time, some socialist and radical feminist theories which characterize the state as an agent of social control and patriarchy have been criticized for being overly deterministic and functional. These theories appear unable to account for why the state should always act in the interests of men, if indeed it does, or why it sometimes implements reforms which weaken the dominant patriarchal order (Gordon 1990, 10). This depiction of the state as a guarantor of patriarchal hegemony, moreover, tends to ignore that public policies often have different consequences for different types of women. In other words, the idea that men have one set of interests and women another set which are merely reflected in the state is an illusion. Interests, as Pringle and Watson maintain, "have to be continuously constructed and reproduced" (Pringle and Watson 1990, 229). Neither can we assume that policies designed to shore up the patriarchal order will, in fact, achieve this outcome. Public policies and state regulation may be very contradictory or have the unintended effect of empowering women to take political action (Chunn 1995, 177).

These and other concerns have lead some feminists to abandon the project of realizing a theory of the state altogether. Australian feminist, Judith Allen, for example, discourages feminists from wasting any more time trying to construct "grand theories" of the state because, she argues, it is "a category of abstraction that is too aggregative, too unitary and too unspecific to be of much use in addressing the disaggregated, diverse and specific (or local) sites that must be of most pressing concern to feminists." Indeed, she goes on to suggest that the state is not an "indigenous category" in feminist theory (Allen 1990, 22).

Allen is, in part, arguing against grand theorizing which conceptualizes the state abstractly as a coherent form resting on pre-given structures like the capitalist system or patriarchal relations. She and others suggest that it is better to study the state as "a set of arenas" reflecting a plurality of often contradictory interests and discourses (Pringle and Watson 1990, 229). Allen's critique, however, also provides a new twist to a long-standing anti-statist tradition within feminist theory and practice. This tradition effectively forfeits to men the realm of mainstream politics, advocates electing instead to get on with the practical matters of women's everyday lives. The strategic implications of whether women choose to mainstream or to disengage from official politics is an important one—one which I believe is more critical at certain political conjunctures than at others (Adamson, Briskin, and McPhail 1988). As feminists, we must constantly ask ourselves whether we risk too much and forfeit strategic political terrain when we choose to ignore or dismiss, in theory or practice, the relevance of the state, especially during a period of fundamental restructuring.

Although many feminist theories of the state appear fatally flawed, the fact remains that there is no feminist space outside of "politics," including mainstream "official" politics. Most feminist concerns—whether relating to health, equity, security—are necessarily state-centred (Brown 1992). Can we really give up the important project of coming to a better strategic understanding of the relationship between public policy and feminist goals of equality by discounting the very political actors and public spaces that are dismantling the gains that the women's movement achieved in the past two decades? When we stand on the outside looking in do we not simply confirm the identities that the state conveys on us, including invisibility, instead of challenging them (Yeatman 1993, 231, 233)?

Rather than turning away from the state as something alien to us, feminists might be better advised to ask what is it about our thinking about the state that fails to capture our experience or to allow us a place for strategic (and defensive) intervention. What's wrong with thinking about the state, for example, as a thing, system, or subject (Brown 1992, 12); as sovereign; as a place where power is centred; as situated above and acting on society; or as an agent of domination which reproduces the hegemony of a single interest, be it capital or patriarchy? What is it about these assumptions that has made the state "the major casualty of recent social theory," especially feminist theory (Pringle and Watson 1992, 54)?

WOMEN AND THE WELFARE STATE

Feminist thinking about the state often has been limited to the gendered underpinnings of the postwar welfare state. Linda Gordon has reviewed this stream of feminist scholarship and has shown that is has moved through three separate stages.

- Discriminatory theories demonstrated how welfare programs acted to reinforce sexist arrangements in domestic and public life.
- Structural theories emphasized how welfare policies functioned both to hold women in a subordinate position in relation to men and as a broader agent of social control. The design of the postwar welfare system ensured women's economic dependence on men and men's economic dependence on wages.
- Women's political activism and influence theory has rejected the idea that all women are necessarily passive victims of the welfare state. Instead, this approach emphasizes how women were active participants in the creation of that state and are empowered by it (Gordon, 1990, 18-23; Andrew 1984).

This latter perspective is an elaboration of the "power resources" approach to the study of the welfare state. This school emphasizes that "politics matter." It rejects the idea that the welfare state is a coherent and instrumental agent of social control—the public patriarch. Instead, social policy is seen to have both a regulatory and emancipatory potential for women, even if the latter is sometimes unintentional (Orloff 1993, 305). Frances Fox Piven is perhaps one of the most insistent on the emancipatory potential of the welfare state for women. Contrary to the deterministic characterization of the state which sees it exercising social control over women and supplanting patriarchal relations of the family with a patriarchal relationship with the state, she argues that the flow of political power is not necessarily always one-sided (Fox Piven 1990, 255).

> Income supports, social services, and government employment partly offset the deteriorating position of women in the family and economy and have even given women a measure of protection and therefore power in the family and economy. In these ways the state is turning out to be the main recourse for women. (Fox Piven 1990, 254)

While many have applauded Fox Piven and like-minded feminists for resisting the all too frequent tendency to depict women as passive victims, the women's political activism approach also has its detractors. Wendy Brown, for example, questions whether the institutions of the welfare state necessarily produce only active political subjects. She suggests instead that, although the welfare state may liberate a woman from the isolation and oppression of the family, "she is immediately colonized and administered by one or more dimensions of masculinist state power" (Brown 1992, 30).

Brown holds this view because she is wary of the immense regulatory capacities of the welfare state and argues that the state both reacts to and actively creates its subjects. She explains that the "state does not simply handle clients or employ staff." It also produces state subjects who are "bureaucratized, dependent, disciplined and gendered" (ibid.).

Brown, like Allen, views the welfare state not as a thing but, instead, a "multifaceted ensemble of power relations," an "unbounded terrain of powers and techniques," and "an ensemble of discourses, rules and practices" (ibid., 12). In the end, however, her analysis remains locked within western feminist debates about the value of the welfare state for women and continues to depict it as responding to a unitary and ahistorical interest— "masculinist state power." Nevertheless, these critiques of feminist theorizing about the welfare state open a window to viewing the state differently, as a complex set of "interrelated but distinct institutions, relations, hierarchies and discourses"—in other words, as an historically specific cultural-political matrix of power relations (Watson 1990, 10).

State as Cultural Form

> There are many different kinds of states—spatially and historically—and each has its own combination of institutions, apparatuses, and arenas which have their own histories, contradictions and relations. (Pringle and Watson 1990, 229)

The tendency to view societal institutions as "reified monoliths" which perpetually victimize women has lost much of its force in the recent years. Many social scientists now view the societal institutions, including those within the state system, as social constructs which reflect the constraints of particular social structures and historical developments (Chunn 1995, 177). A social constructionist lens neither denies that the state is constantly implicated in the production and reproduction of power relations, nor that its policies have real effects on the everyday lives of women. Neither does it deny that the state acts instrumentally (too often consistently) in the interests of some and not others. It does, however, challenge the way feminists have traditionally understood the dynamic between state power, gender identity, and gender relations (Brodie 1994). As Orloff puts it, the new feminist thinking about the state emphasizes how public policy and, in particular, social welfare policy affects "women's material situations, shapes gender relationships, structures political conflict and participation, and contributes to the formation and mobilization of specific identities and interests" (Orloff 1993, 303). In other words, women, as a category of social actors, do not stand outside of a particular state formation but, instead, are actively shaped by public policy and other cultural forms.

The vast array of public policies and regulations which emanate from the state help shape our life chances, our most intimate relationships, what we believe to be political, who we think we are, and how we make claims on the state and for what. This is what Corrigan and Sayer are pointing to when they argue that we must "grasp state forms culturally." They suggest that the time-worn idea of the state as a coherent unity positioned instrumentally above society is "in large part an ideological construct, a fiction" (Corrigan and Sayer 1985, 3). While the institutions of government are real enough, the state-society relation is less directive than coterminous and discursive, and is embedded in our shared understandings at any point of what is natural, neutral, and universal. Corrigan and Sayer suggest that these shared understandings are anything but natural, neutral, and universal. They are simply "impositional claims"—assertions about reality which are self-interested, biased, historically-specific, and thus subject to political contestation. Impositional claims, nonetheless, provide the cultural foundations affecting the kind of state that governs a particular society.

Different state forms, whether they be laissez-faire, welfare, or neoliberal, weave different meanings into our everyday lives. Among other things, these meanings are enshrined in law and public policy, embedded in institutions, and enforced through regulation and sanction (Corrigan and Sayer 1985, 2-7). States, first and foremost, "state."

> (States) define, in great detail, acceptable forms and images of social activity and individual and collective identity; they regulate, in empirically specifiable ways . . . social life. In this sense, 'the State' never stops talking. (Corrigan and Sayer 1985, 3)

The idea that feminists can view the state as a complex, historical and cultural form directs our attention to dominant discourses, the impositional claims, and the creation of particular kinds of political agents. "Discourse" is admittedly an illusive concept. For our purposes, we can think about it as a set of impositional claims which attempts to make politically contestable positions appear to be non-political and uncontestable—part of the natural order of things. Politics is characterized by conflicting discourses, each of which puts into "play a privileged set of viewpoints," making certain thoughts and ideas present and others absent (Eisenstein 1988, 10). The significance of discourses in political analysis, however, reaches beyond the mere play of competing ideas and the interests that they advance. During any historical period, some discourses prevail over others and thereby have a greater influence in shaping our political reality at that time. Such discourses help us interpret our social relations and institutions, what we consider to be a social problem and its appropriate remedies, where the sphere of political negotiation begins and ends, and who we believe we are. They provide the foundations of a "particular historical form of social order" (Corrigan and Sayer 1985, 4).

The concepts of discourse and of the state as an historical cultural form, then, invite us to investigate how states and political identities have been "stated" by different states and how these particular social constructions enforce relations of domination and political conflict. Among the most critical impositional claims that the liberal democratic state has stated and restated throughout its long history has been the appropriate boundaries between the public, the market, and the domestic spheres. As the next section of this chapter argues, this historical negotiation of boundaries is critical both to understanding the political subordination and struggles of women and the women's movement, and to decoding the impositional claims of the emerging new order.

LIBERAL DEMOCRACY AND THE PUBLIC/PRIVATE DIVIDE

> Liberal democracy designates certain areas as outside of government control, sometimes by formally establishing individual rights and freedoms in a written constitution but more commonly through historically shifting conventions over what can be considered a public concern. Whichever procedure operates the arm of government will be limited and kept away from the private domain. (Anne Phillips 1991, 15)

Liberal states were initially conceived and have been repeatedly restructured through what Walzer appropriately terms, "the art of separation" (Walzer 1984, 315). Early European liberal theorists sought to reconfigure feudal society, which rested on impositional claims about natural hierarchies, interdependence, and the organic whole, by recasting it as a "world of walls." Emerging alongside capitalism, liberalism recast the old feudal order as a segmented society—"they drew lines, marked off different realms and created the sociopolitical map" (ibid.) with which, although many times altered, we still live. The church was separated from the state so that it could be governed by the principles of responsible government and, later, liberal democracy. In turn, the state was mapped out as a separate sphere from the market which operated under the rules of laissez-faire capitalism, creating a profoundly unequal and oppressive class system. And, finally, a line was drawn between the public and the domestic which was subject to the rule of individual men (ibid.).

Classic liberal discourse prescribed and then materialized in the reorganization of metaphorical, economic, and political space. At its heart was a new set of impositional claims about what was natural and universal, what was naturally on and off the political agenda, and the rules and distributional practices that were applicable to the public world of liberal-democratic politics, the private market sector, and the domestic sphere of the family. It pronounced a "natural" and, therefore, politically uncontestable complementarity between social spaces and social relations, as well as between institutions and functions. The success of the new social order depended on keeping each of these spheres separated at least at the level of shared beliefs. Each sphere was to be governed by different rules, hierarchies, and distributive practices (Bowles and Gintis 1986, 98-101).

In these separations, liberalism reorganized the framework through which social power was expressed. It put sovereignty in the hands of a new social actor—the citizen—who exercised limited power through the institutions of liberal democracy such as responsible government and, later, democratic elections. At the same time, however, classic liberalism profoundly contracted political space and the legitimate objects of political struggle. The combined doctrines of laissez-faire capitalism and the negative state freed the market from political intervention. The role of the negative state in the economy was largely limited to enforcing the rights of private property and the legality of the contract. Similarly, the public/domestic divide protected men from the gaze of the state within the family. The realm of the private and personal was sacred ground upon which the state could not tread. Often women were isolated in the home and subject to the rule of men. A man's home was indeed "his castle" (Pateman 1988, 192).

> There is an elemental connection between the pattern of gender relations and the way the state is constituted as a specific institution in social life. (Fransway, Court, and Connell 1989, 6)

Feminists have long argued that liberalism's public/domestic partition was and continues to be crucial to understanding oppressive gender relations. Although presented as a universal, neutral, and natural way of ordering social relations, this division was deeply gendered and the primary political mechanism in the reproduction of an unequal gender order and the subordination of women (Bowles and Gintis 1986, 66). This powerful social convention imposed a perfect coincidence among function, institution, and gender identity, thereby saturating cultural and political forms with a sexual division of labour. Moreover, those things deemed to be the proper sphere for men—politics and the economy—were valorized over women's proper sphere—the home. Classic liberalism envisioned an artificial and politically negotiated public world, resting on the "natural" world of the family which, if left undisturbed, would satisfy society's reproductive needs. In turn, patriarchal discourse constructed women as "naturally" suited to the family structure, the unpaid domestic work of women as "natural," and the hetero-patriarchal family as a "natural" entity. As Brown puts it, "everywhere nature greets nature" (1992, 27) and, of course, since this organization was natural, it was also impervious to political contestation and intervention. One does not, as the saying goes, argue with Mother Nature! The family and the polis were cast as different, autonomous, and inescapably gendered. Neither women nor most aspects of their daily lives were seen to have a legitimate place in politics. So enduring was this discourse that those opposing women's suffrage at the turn of this century commonly argued that if women had the vote they would lose their femininity and that the home would collapse (Cook and Mitchinson 1976).

It is worth emphasizing here that liberalism's public/private divide is neither fixed, natural, nor obvious but is, instead, a profoundly political mechanism for organizing gender relations and systems of power (Siltanen and Stanworth 1984, 208). The realm of the domestic was and is constituted by a battery of impositional claims, public policies, and practices. It is imbued with political codings that call it private and natural. The idea of the separation of the public and the private sphere, then, is both true and false (Pateman 1992, 226). It is true to the extent that this space and its inhabitants are constructed as being outside the terrain of the political, and false to the extent that this boundary can only be enforced by making it the object of public policies and political struggles (Anne Phillips 1991, 87, 95).

The public/private divide is not, as liberal discourse proposes, the point of separation between the political and the apolitical—the line where politics ends and nature begins. Instead, it is an historically shifting and contested cultural construction which is saturated with political codings and gendered meanings. The public and the private are opposite sides of the same coin and each reinforces the other. That which is deemed to be public is the cultural-political-discursive space upon which different forms of the liberal-democratic state have been built. In turn, these historical state forms do not simply address private needs: they configure, administer, and produce them (Brown 1992, 30). Contrary to liberal discourse, then, the public and the private are not separate worlds but historically shifting and mutually reinforcing realms. The nature and the inhabitants of the domestic sphere are the creation of historical-political decisions and struggles. In other words, as Okin observes, "the very notion that the state can choose whether or not to intervene in family life makes no sense" (Okin 1979, 102). Particular state forms rest on and reinforce equally particular configurations of the private, the domestic, and the family.

CHAPTER THREE

Changing State Forms
and the Women's Movement

THE QUESTION OF BOUNDARIES—OF where to draw the culturally and politically enforced line between the prerogatives of the state, the market, and the family—has informed liberal-democratic politics, in one form or another, since its beginnings. Both workers' and women's organizations have repeatedly engaged in a tug of war with their opponents around the divide between the state and the market, and the state and the home. For the most part, these struggles have revolved around politicizing relations such as, for example, workplace conditions and organization or poverty and gender relations— relations that classic liberalism defined as private concerns. Women, workers, and others have sought to expand the realm of the public and, in so doing, make so-called "private" matters subject to political negotiation and collectiveprovision.

In this chapter I endeavour to make the idea of shifting boundaries between the public and private and the state as a cultural form more concrete by examining the evolution of the public face of the Canadian women's movement during the two separate eras of the laissez-faire state and the Keynesian welfare state. There is some disagreement about when exactly these particular state forms emerged and disappeared. This is because new state forms emerge in bits and pieces often retaining elements of the past while social actors struggle to create new institutions for the future. The shift from one state form to another, in other words, is a prolonged period of restructuring. Canadian political economists have identified three distinct periods of major social transformation in Canada. Each period of restructuring, in turn, generated a unique state form (Brodie 1990). The laissez-faire state, which reigned from approximately the 1840s until the Great Depression of the 1930s, coincided with the development of industrial capitalism. The welfare state, dating from the 1940s until the 1970s, is associated with corporate capitalism and the branch plant economy. The current fashioning of the neoliberal state parallels the ascendency of transnational capitalism (Chunn 1995, 177).

Importantly, these different state forms are also implicated in different configurations of the public and private, of family forms, and of the gender order. Haraway suggests that "although lived problematically and unequally," specific kinds of families are associated with each of these three periods within the history of capitalism and related state forms. She suggests that they can be thought of in the following way:

- the patriarchal family, structured by the dichotomy between the public and private and accompanied by the white bourgeois ideology of separate spheres which provided the foundations for the laissez-faire state;
- the modern family mediated or enforced by the welfare state and conventions like the family wage;
- the present-day family of the "homework" economy with its proliferation of women-headed households (Haraway 1991, 167).

In what follows I link these state and familial forms with the dominant preoccupations of the Canadian women's movement during each period. There are few parallels in the histories of the English and French Canadian women's movement during these years. Unless otherwise stated, then, this chapter examines the first and second waves of the English Canadian women's movement.

THE LAISSEZ-FAIRE STATE AND THE FIRST WAVE

> ... the dichotomy between the public and private
> is ultimately what the feminist movement is all
> about. (Pateman 1989, 118)

The laissez-faire state made women the objects of public policy long before they were officially recognized in law as legitimate political actors (Anne Phillips 1991, 87). It inscribed the private sphere with a particular construction of gender and gender relations which, in time, provided the basis for women's entry into the mainstream of Canadian politics. Women were contained in the home by their being denied legal personhood and citizenship rights while their dependence on men was ensured through a series of restrictions on education, employment, and ownership. Women were simply denied entry into certain fields of education and prestigious professions and the right to control and accumulate their own property.

Married women, in particular, lost their legal visibility through the so-called "unity doctrine." It deemed that a woman was the extension of her husband and, thus, was ascribed an official status comparable to that of an infant or an institutionalized incompetent (Chunn 1995, 179). This construction of all women as private and dependent was rigidly inscribed in law yet, paradoxically, these conditions were widely understood as part of the natural order of things. In fact, women who were not dependent on individual men or who fought for the legal recognition of women as citizens in their own right were judged to be decidedly unfeminine.

> What complicates the situation is that the persons who are appealing for the votes (for women) are of higher intelligence, but with shallower instincts, than the average of the sex to which they apparently belong. They are not typical. They belong to a higher, a more masculine, type. (Anti-suffrage campaigner Andrew Macphail 1914, quoted in Cook and Mitchinson 1976, 304)

The public/private partition was imbued with gender codings from its conception and it has left lasting inscriptions on women as political actors. Initially, only men could become citizens and claim the liberal rights of freedom and equality in the public sphere while women were deemed the natural subjects of men in the private sphere. For most of its reign, the laissez-faire state constructed women as "pre-political" subjects—a public excluded from "the public" (Chapman 1993). The rigid boundary between the public and private served to constrain and limit the terrain of politics, enclaving and shielding gender issues and relations from political contestation and negotiation (Fraser 1989). Women's political subordination was made to appear as part of the natural order of things. More than this, terms and behaviours which were deemed appropriate in the public sphere, such as equality, liberty, and democracy, were treated as incompatible, indeed as threats to the very workings of the family.

> The question whether it is desirable that women should take part in politics is closely connected with those relating to their domestic and industrial position. It is a question not as to the relative intelligence or virtue of the two sexes, but whether politics are or can be women's sphere. . . . The

> disqualification (of women) . . . is not one of
> intellect but of position. (Goldwin Smith 1872,
> quoted in Cook and Mitchinson 1976, 34)

Women's enfranchisement (by 1921) and winning legal recognition as persons (the Person's Case, 1929) are sometimes recounted as historic mileposts for Canadian women in their long march toward gender equality. This perspective, however, largely misrepresents the Canadian women's movement during the period and how women initially entered liberal democratic politics in Canada. Canadian women were not called into the public on the same basis as men—as members of a gender neutral community of citizens. Admittedly, a small number of the early English Canadian feminists did struggle for the equal treatment of the sexes in all aspects of life. The Toronto Women's Literary Club, for example, was founded in 1876 with the expressed purpose of agitating for women's political rights. These early equal-rights feminists, however, were overshadowed by both the dominant currents of the Canadian women's movement and the turn-of-the-century social reform movement.

Maternal feminists, housed within organizations such as the Women's Christian Temperance Union (WCTU) founded in 1891, the National Council of Women (NCW) started in 1893, and the Young Women's Christian Association (YWCA), dominated the first wave of Canadian feminism. Unlike equal-rights feminists, they celebrated rather than challenged prevailing patriarchal family forms and representations of women (Ursel 1992, 80-82). These early maternal feminists and the anti-feminists of the period shared very similar understandings about who women were and about the gendered organization of the private sphere. Women belonged in the home and it was from there that all good women—daughters, wives, and especially mothers—exercised their inherent moral superiority. The question of whether women could exercise their special qualities in the public realm without contaminating themselves through their political participation was the major point of dispute among suffragists and anti-suffragists.

Constructed as the moral guardians of the nation, first wave feminists soon became the obvious ally of the Victorian social reform movement. This powerful coalition of (white, protestant, middle-class) social reformers was concerned with what they saw as a decaying social fabric due to rapid industrialization and urbanization, and heavy inflows of non-Anglo-Saxon immigrants. In contrast to the much idealized rural community, the cities of turn-of-the-century Canada were not particularly pleasant places to live, especially for the working class and the poor. Housing, health facilities, and sanitation were inadequate while women and children filled unregulated industrial "sweat-shops."

The Victorian social reform movement considered all of these problems as a threat to society, especially to its bedrock—the family. The early social reformers thus sought to rebuild urban Canada by protecting the family through such things as state regulation of working hours and conditions for women and children, public education, housing and product standards, and public sanitation. The early feminists gained political currency within the social reform movement precisely because they wanted things previously encoded as the ideal "private"—for example, temperance, sanitation, the nurturing of children, the protection of women—to be "a model for the public" (Jenson 1990a, 12). As historian Susan Mann (Trofimenkoff) recounts of the first wave of Canadian feminism, "When [feminists] took on public tasks beyond the home, they did so to protect the home. They were merely enlarging their maternal sphere for the benefit of society" (Trofimenkoff 1983, 199).

> Enfranchisement (in other countries) has led neither to divided households nor divided skirts. On the contrary, family life has been strengthened with a new sympathy....Temperance, morality, justice, and high principles, more influence and the passage and enforcement of humanitarian laws is more vigorously demanded and jealously watched. (Mrs. Gordon Grant to a WCTU meeting 1888, quoted in Cook and Mitchinson 1976, 264)

The first wave of the English Canadian women's movement defined women in a manner consistent with the dominant patriarchal vision of the gender order. Maternal feminists did not envision themselves as genderless citizens of the laissez-faire state who, like men, were entitled to abstract citizenship rights. Instead, they were invited into the political arena as gendered citizens who embodied dominant impositional claims about the public/private divide and the appropriate gender order. It was by virtue of their womanhood, and their moral superiority and social consciousness, that they were recommended for citizenship rights. In turn, the male political elite was willing to accept women as voters in order to reinforce the existing gender order and the patriarchal family form. Women would use the vote instrumentally to clean up politics and society and save the family. In so doing, the first wave of the Canadian women's movement reinforced rather than challenged the rigid division between the public and private, upon which the laissez-faire state rested, and helped to perpetuate the structured dependency of women within marriage (Chunn 1995, 140).

Jenson argues that these women came quite late to the realization that their reformism required that they be voting citizens (1990a). Their alliance with the Victorian social reform movement was fruitful, nonetheless, both because the social reform movement supported the idea of women's suffrage and because it permitted the early feminists to reasonably expect that they would see their social reforms implemented (Ursel 1992, 82). If this alliance reinforced patriarchy, it was also very strategic. It granted the women's movement the political power that it needed to enact its reforms. The early years of this century saw a raft of social reform legislation enacted, although most of this legislation was regulatory rather than redistributive in nature. Among other things, the reforms included restrictions on child labour, selective protection for women workers, the setting of a minimum wage for unmarried women, a series of regulations on women's reproduction, consumer protection measures, the legal obligation for men to support their wives and children and, in the case of death or desertion, provisions for state support for destitute women and children (Ursel 1992, 36-7; Chunn,1995, 185).

Women used the vote to protect the domestic sphere but, as some have noted, these initiatives also served to erode the laissez-faire state's rigid division between the public and private and set the stage for the emergence of the postwar welfare state (Burt 1994, 207). In a sense, the inclusion of the domestic within the jurisdiction of the laissez-faire state eroded its very foundations and marked the beginnings of its demise. But it also marked the end of the first wave of Canadian feminism. Once its reform agenda had been achieved and women had gained citizenship rights, there was little left to sustain the momentum of the first wave of the women's movement. Women's groups such as the WCTU, the NCW, and the YWCA continued to thrive but the overtly political side of the first wave faded from public view.

The minority of Canadian women who did enter the official realm of liberal democratic politics were integrated into political parties through the creation of women's auxiliaries—gendered appendages to the main (men's) party organizations. The first national auxiliary, the Federation of Liberal Women of Canada, was launched in 1928. The Conservative Party soon followed suit by creating its own women's auxiliary. These organizations quickly spread to the constituency organizations of both major federal parties, thereby firmly entrenching a sexual division of labour within the party system. Auxiliaries provided a ready pool of dedicated women volunteers during election campaigns and succeeded in keeping women out of the main party organizations where the power rested. They continued to function in this manner until the 1970s (Brodie 1985; Gotell and Brodie 1991, 56).

THE WELFARE STATE AND SECOND WAVE FEMINISM

During the immediate post-World War II period a distinctly Canadian variant of the Keynesian welfare state (KWS) came to occupy and politicize many of the spaces that laissez-faire liberalism previously had declared to be unalterably, naturally, and universally private. The emergence of the welfare state was another instance of restructuring during which the boundaries between the economy and state and the public and the domestic were fundamentally realigned (Brodie 1994). The welfare state realized a radical expansion of the public through direct intervention in the economy, and by subjecting the family and other aspects of private life to new forms of state scrutiny and assistance (Andrew 1984, 667; Abbott and Wallace 1992, 17). This new state form was, in part, an elaboration of the visions of the Victorian social reform movement. More important, it represented a compromise with oppositional movements such as organized labour, the social gospel movement, and fabian socialists that gained force in Canadian politics during the Great Depression of the 1930s and the war years. The welfare state was grounded on new impositional claims about the proper role of the state and the rights of citizens.

Ursel calls this new understanding "welfare ideology" and argues that it was "an achievement of public consensus equal in significance, but substantially different to the Victorian social reform movement" (Ursel 1992, 205). The Canadian welfare state was built up incrementally and afforded Canadians fewer protections than some of its European counterparts. Nevertheless, the prewar idea of a means-tested welfare was replaced with the concept of social security for all citizens as a universal right (ibid., 206). The welfare state advanced a new collective understanding about the public and the private and about the rights of citizens. Principal among these were the claims:

- that economic activity should be collectively regulated in order to maximize the collective welfare;
- that citizens had a right to have some basic needs met by the state, especially when private mechanisms failed;
- of a commitment to formal equality and impersonal procedure (Young 1990, 67).

The welfare state also altered the constitution of the gender order and women's place within it. The new order rested on a very particular model of the workplace and the home. It presumed a stable working/middle-class nuclear family supported by a male breadwinner, a dependent wife and children, and the unpaid domestic labour of women. The state guaranteed through the protection collective bargaining and welfare measures that there

39

would be a "family wage." It measured the income needed for an individual male worker to support a family. A woman's paid labour was thereby deemed unnecessary or, failing that, secondary to that of her husband. The family wage and the dependent homemaker were only two of the cultural forms supported and reinforced by the Keynesian welfare state (McDowell 1991, 400-2).

If the KWS reinforced a particular kind of family and gender order, it also created new political spaces for women. It viewed women as a different kind of political actor with different claims on the state. Instead of casting women as the moral force of politics, the KWS largely spoke to women as mothers framed within the context of a nuclear family headed by a male wage-earner. After the war, women were actively encouraged, if not forced, to leave the workforce and return to the home and all the unpaid domestic labour that this entailed. Feminist state theorists are quite correct in identifying the discourses around welfare and its provisions as central to the construction of the gender order and women's subordination during the postwar years (Pringle and Watson 1990, 235). The new welfare ideology shifted the emphasis of state discourse and practice from regulation of the workplace and the family to the administration of income and social services for the family.

The Family Allowance Act (1944, i.e., mother's allowance) was one of Canada's first universal social welfare programs. It was also somewhat unique among social security measures considering that its major beneficiaries— mothers—never campaigned for it and that it was unanimously endorsed by all parties in the House of Commons (Ursel 1992, 190, 205). The major debate about mother's allowance, in fact, revolved around religion and ethnicity. Some Honourable Members felt that it would encourage Quebeckers and Catholics to have more babies. This argument was obviously bigoted but it also missed the point. The baby bonus was designed to shore up the family wage. And, this welfare provision recognized women primarily as mothers and not as ethnics. The welfare state readily transferred money from single working women who did not fit the dominant cultural model to women who did, that is, to mothers (Pringle and Watson 1990, 236). In a very real sense, then, welfare policy was less directed at women as a social category than *through* mothers in order to reinforce a particular family form and the postwar organization of the labour force and the economy.

> The welfare state is not just a set of services, it is also a set of ideas about society, about the family and, not the least, about women who have a centrally important role within the family, as its linchpin. (Wilson 1977, 9)

The family was differently constituted under the welfare state, opening up for policy consideration and political negotiation many aspects of the everyday which previously had been considered as private and, as such, incompatible with political intervention. In the process, new public spaces for women were opened, but these spaces usually rested on the assumption, initially at least, that "women's interests" and "family interests" were one and the same. There was little recognition that the family could be a site of political conflict for women and a primary site of women's subordination. However circumscribed, these new political spaces did enable Canadian women to organize, to make political claims, to lobby the state for better services for the family, and, eventually, to demand state action to improve the condition of women in all aspects of their lives. In other words, the welfare state, resting as it did on its particular negotiation of the public and private, became a political resource, albeit an ambiguous one, for women. They were allowed, enabled, and encouraged to make claims "as women," although ultimately it was white, middle-class women who had the loudest voice.

The welfare state provided space for the growth of a myriad of women's organizations, often state-financed, that shaped a collective identity and increasingly drew the overtly political arm of the women's movement into new state-centred "progressive" coalitions. Importantly, these developments forged a strong bond between the English Canadian women's movement and the federal government. In contrast, the lines of coalition in Québec were more commonly established among the women's movement, Québec nationalists, and the provincial state, particularly after the Quiet Revolution of the 1960s transformed and secularized the provincial state and the delivery of social services (Lamoureux 1987). As Fraser puts it, the welfare state brought new forms of social control *as well as* new forms of conflict, new social movements, and new conflict zones (Fraser 1989, 132). Within the specific context of Canadian politics, this meant that the emergent second wave of the women's movement in Québec and the rest of Canada would follow quite different paths and look to different places within the federal state structure to advance their shared goal of gender equality. The women's movements in Québec and English Canada were created and subsequently matured within the context of the "two solitudes" (Begin 1992, 23).

THE ROYAL COMMISSION ON THE STATUS OF WOMEN

In its early years, the second wave of the Canadian women's movement took a variety of different forms ranging from intimate consciousness-raising groups and radical and socialist feminist collectives to rape crisis centres and equality-seeking groups (Adamson, Briskin, and McPhail 1988). Most commentators, however, trace the development of its most public face to the establishment of the Royal Commission of the Status of Women (RCSW) in 1967. The idea of establishing such a commission had been contemplated by many English Canadian women's groups for a number of years, especially after a similar task force was appointed in the United States during the Kennedy administration. In 1966, English Canada's Committee on Equality (CEW), a temporary grouping of over thirty women's groups, joined forces with the newly formed Fédération des femmes du Québec to demand that the federal government establish a royal commission to investigate the status of women in Canadian society and to recommend policy responses (Begin 1992, 23-5). The Pearson government responded positively six months later by appointing the Royal Commission on the Status of Women under the direction of journalist Florence Bird. The government directed the commission to "recommend what steps might be taken by the Federal Government to ensure for women equal opportunities with men in all aspects of Canadian society" (Canada, 1970 vii; Findlay 1987, 34-5).

It took the RCSW three years to complete its *Report* and another two years before the federal government gave it lukewarm approval "in principle." The commission made 167 recommendations, some 122 of which were defined exclusively as federal responsibilities (Findlay 1988, 5-6). These recommendations, however, did not reflect an overtly feminist subtext. Monique Begin, who worked for the commission, recounts that it lacked a "general theory of women's oppression" and did not have "a feminist analysis of the family" (Begin 1992, 31). Instead, the commission applied an equal opportunity framework which depicted women's subordination as a problem of inadequate access, unwarranted discrimination, and a lack of education (Findlay 1987, 33). This absence of an explicitly feminist analysis reflected both the theoretical underdevelopment of the fledgling movement and the distance of the commission from that movement.

> The commission did not benefit from discussions generated within the women's movement because we did not know what was going on, except through rare public demonstrations. . . . These were often quite radical and difficult to understand from outside the movement and without the help of written manifestos. (Begin 1992, 28)

RCSW is widely recognized as having set the political agenda for the women's movement, especially in English Canada during the 1970s and beyond (Burt 1986). It identified "the problems" and offered practical solutions for federal government intervention in most sectors of Canadian society. In a sense, it was quite compatible with popular assumptions about the propriety and assumed effectiveness of state intervention. As important, it provided a checklist around which the women's movement could mobilize for immediate action and measure the federal government's progress toward women's equality.

The RCSW directly influenced the politics and strategies of the women's movement. During these early years, feminists were often divided by debates concerning whether it was better to work for change inside the system—the so-called "liberal feminist" "mainstream" position—or to struggle outside the mainstream in order to avoid co-optation and to bring about a complete transformation of the system itself. This latter strategy was more often advocated by radical and socialist feminists. The timing of the royal commission, coming as it did in the early years of the second wave, served to strengthen the liberal feminist position.

One of the less visible outcomes of the RCSW, then, was that a majority of women came to believe that the government would respond to their concerns. At least initially, the second wave of English Canadian feminism tended to view the state as a neutral agent which could correct the systemic biases that prevented women from achieving equality with men. And, as Vickers suggests, this attitude toward the state "probably best explains the willingness of many women's groups, however apparently radical, to receive state funding" (Vickers 1992, 45). During the 1970s, then, the women's movement behaved very much as a lobby group in Ottawa. Feminists began to develop their expertise in many policy fields, particularly social welfare, and to adopt formal lobbying skills. In the process, "liberal feminism became the 'public face' of the women's movement" (Findlay 1988, 6-7).

The Royal Commission on the Status of Women was also instrumental in providing the rationale for the very formation of key representational institutions for women both inside and outside the federal bureaucracy. The early 1970s brought a proliferation within the federal government of offices and agencies designed to improve some aspect of women's lives. Among these were the Women's Bureau in the Department of Labour, the Office of Equal Opportunity in the Public Service Commission, the Office of the Co-ordinator of the Status of Women in the Privy Council Office, the Canadian Advisory Council on the Status of Women (CACSW), the appointment of a Minister Responsible for the Status of Women within the federal cabinet and, most important, the Women's Program in the Citizenship Branch of the Secretary of State. The government mandated the Women's Program to pursue "the development of a society in which the full potential of women as citizens is recognized and utilized" (Burt 1994, 216). This mandate reflected the prevailing governing philosophy at the time that state funding of disadvantaged groups would both enhance Canadian democracy and enrich the policy-making process (Pal 1993). Guided by this new thinking, federal funding for the Women's Program multiplied throughout the 1970s and early 1980s growing from a meagre $223,000 in 1973 to $12.4 million in 1987. These funds enabled women's groups of all varieties to establish offices and pursue special projects (Burt 1994, 216).

THE NATIONAL ACTION COMMITTEE
ON THE STATUS OF WOMEN

The RCSW encouraged the consolidation of women's organizations outside the federal government. In 1972, the Strategy for Change Conference saw the formation of second-wave feminism's key frontline organization, the National Action Committee on the Status of Women (NAC). This conference as well as the founding of NAC reflected a collective resolve that an organization outside the federal government was needed in order to pressure policy-makers to implement the recommendations of the Royal Commission (Findlay 1987, 37-39).

During the 1970s, NAC and other women's organizations repeatedly lobbied state actors to expand the social welfare system and to make it more responsive to their conception of women's needs. And the federal government appeared to respond, especially after International Women's Year in 1975. In these years, which Findlay identifies as the "consultative period," the federal government invited the organized women's movement to consult on a broad range of issues ranging from pay equity to rape to divorce reform (Findlay 1988, 7). This consultation strategy produced reforms, but, what is more important is that it won many converts within the women's movement. It strengthened the English Canadian women's movement's gaze on the federal state.

> Such affirmations of political commitment to improve the status of women in Canada were sufficient to win new allies to the liberal feminists' view that the women's movement must tailor its strategies to work with the state in a collaborative and consultative manner. (Findlay 1988, 7)

Throughout the 1970s, then, the dominant target of the women's movement and NAC, its most important umbrella organization, was the state, specifically the national government. Most Canadian feminists saw "the state more as a provider of services, including the service of regulation, than as a reinforcer of patriarchal norms, and most seem[ed] to believe that services, whether child care or medicare, [would] help" (Vickers 1992, 45).

In turn, the organized women's movement was increasingly recognized as a legitimate lobby group which was entitled to consultation in the policy-making process, worthy of gender-designated funding and programs, and able to access strategic points within the federal bureaucracy. In the process, the women's movement became a recognized actor in federal politics as a representative of a social category with a distinct interest in the postwar welfare state. Indeed, by the early 1980s, women's organizations found themselves increasingly entangled in the federal government's political agenda, "working hand in hand," as Findlay puts it, "to implement its commitment to the status of women" (1988, 7).

The constitutional politics of the early 1980s only served to strengthen this relationship, although this outcome was far from certain during the protracted constitutional negotiations which culminated with the entrenchment of the Charter of Rights and Freedoms in the Canadian constitution. Achieving constitutional protection for sexual equality was a significant achievement for Canadian women. Women first mobilized to protest the use of the wording contained within the Canadian Bill of Rights which they successfully argued had proven to be an inadequate protection for women's rights. After this initial struggle, the federal government appeared to be a strong supporter of constitutional guarantees for sexual equality. Its motivations, however, were not entirely principled. It was trying to build public support, wherever it could find it, for its unilateral constitutional initiatives and for the Charter of Rights and Freedoms to counter the objections of the provincial governments that saw the Charter as a threat to the legislative powers guaranteed them in the British North America Act (BNA). The women's movement, however, was soon shocked to discover that, after months of pressure, the Trudeau government was prepared to make the constitutional guarantee of sexual equality subject to the override clause. In other words, it appeared ready to allow provincial governments the option of opting out of these equality guarantees. As Gotell suggests, some provinces demanded the weakening of the sexual equality clause as the price for their support of the constitutional package (1993, 198). A massive lobbying effort ensued and the sexual equality clause was finally placed beyond the reach of the notwithstanding clause in the Charter.

This episode was an expansive moment in the history of the women's movement in English Canada, both mobilizing many women who had never before been part of the women's movement and providing a sense of empowerment to women's organizations. It also gave impetus to organizations such as the Legal and Education Action Fund (LEAF), which successfully convinced the federal government that the women's movement needed financial support, in the form of the Court Challenges Program, to pursue women's rights in the Courts (Gotell 1993). This enthusiasm in the English

Canadian women's movement for the potential of the Charter, however, was not shared by the Québécois women's movement. Alongside other groups in the province, it viewed the Charter as a betrayal of Québec and a threatening federal imposition on provincial powers. The 1980-82 constitutional episode, in other words, provided yet another illustration of how the women's movement inside and outside Québec was a product of and interacted within quite distinct political contexts and political/institutional matrices.

By the mid-1980s, the English Canadian women's movement approached the apex of its influence within the federal government. During the 1984 election campaign, for example, NAC was obviously perceived to hold enough influence among women voters that the three major parties agreed to participate in a NAC-sponsored federal leadership debate on women's issues (Brodie 1985). The early 1980s witnessed a previously undocumented shift in the behaviour of women voters—the emergence of a gender gap. Public opinion polls, both then and now, show that women tend to be more sympathetic than men to social welfare issues. What was different about the early 1980s was that women appeared to be mobilizing in federal politics as a distinctive bloc of voters favouring the Liberal party by a margin of almost 10 percent (Gotell and Brodie 1991, 63).

> The spectacle of three men, who at best had only a nodding acquaintance with women's issues before the debate, being heavily briefed by the women in the party in order to debate each other on how women would be best treated by their own party, was an historic first that feminists thoroughly enjoyed. (Cohen 1992, 23)

Despite these very real public manifestations of political power, it is important to emphasize that the legitimacy of the women's movement during these years was almost entirely attached to its ability to speak to "women's issues." Within the context of the welfare state, this effectively meant social policy matters alone. As Marjorie Cohen, a feminist economist long active in NAC recounts, by "the 1980s government and employers had accepted women's intervention in issues like equal pay, maternity leave, and the movement of women out of traditional occupations. They also accepted our right to speak on daycare, reproductive choice, pornography—anything that could be seen as a women's issue" (Cohen 1992, 217). Later in the decade, when the women's movement began to discuss issues lying outside of a narrow definition of social policy (issues which nonetheless had devastating implications for social policy) such as macro-economic policy, their interventions were interpreted as inappropriate. Cohen observes that women's contributions to these broader debates were always treated "as a discussion of welfare policy, not economic policy" (Cohen 1992, 218).

> ... (when) we began to talk about economic issues like the budget, trade policy, privatization, deregulation, and the general structure of the Canadian economy, we were going to far. These were not women's issues: women were not "experts" and therefore our criticism had little credibility. (Cohen 1992, 218-19)

So long as the welfare state remained unchallenged, the organized women's movement could and did expand its sphere of influence, particularly inside the federal state itself. This, however, was not to continue. As described in Chapter 1, the mid-1980s saw a breakdown in the postwar consensus about the role of the Keynesian state, the federal government and its welfare ideology. After a decade of "restructuring," with its attendant shifts in discourse and state form, it has become increasingly apparent that the very political spaces within which the contemporary women's movement found much of its cohesion and empowerment are disappearing. Social welfarism is rapidly being displaced by an, as yet, unfinished political struggle about the very meaning of the public and private. The women's movement, as with other oppositional movements, is only now coming to terms with the cultural dimensions of restructuring. The women's movement did not simply face a hostile federal government between 1984 and 1993; it became embedded in a process of carving out a new consensus, a new cultural ethos, and a new state form (Yeatman 1990, 101). Chapter Four describes this new ethos. Chapter Five explores how this new ethos has challenged the second wave of the women's movement.

Setting the Foundations
for the Neoliberal State

MICHEL FOUCAULT ONCE SUGGESTED THAT "the state consists in the codification of a whole number of power relations" and that a "revolution is a different type of codification of these same relations" (quoted in Held et al. 1983, 312-13). Canada, similar to all western democracies, is currently undergoing just such a revolution—one that is still incomplete and subject to contestation. This revolution seeks to recode the realm of the political which the Keynesian welfare state "stated" in the postwar years with new shared understandings about what is natural and desirable. This chapter examines how the emerging new state form—the neoliberal state—is progressively changing the terrain of the political, the workplace, and the home and, thus, is reshaping gender relations and the everyday lives of Canadian women.

SHRINKING THE PUBLIC: EXPANDING THE PRIVATE
Market Driven Adjustment
The emergence of the neoliberal state is being driven by what I term "restructuring discourse" (Brodie 1994; 1995). This discourse seeks to radically shrink the realm of political negotiation by increasing the autonomy of market forces and of the family. The central theme of restructuring discourse is that we have no political choices left about how to shape our collective lives and future other than to follow a market-driven approach to the globalization of the international economy. We are told that there is simply no escaping "adjustment," which restructuring discourse defines exclusively as reducing fiscal and regulatory burdens on business and lowering expectations about the role of the state. The contention that there

49

is no choice was the primary rationale offered to Canadians for entering both CUFTA and NAFTA.

> There is no alternative. (Margaret Thatcher)

More recently, the no-choice metaphor has been directed at the ballooning deficit and government spending, particularly in the realm of social policy. The chief executive of the Canadian Imperial Bank of Commerce, who earns $1.5 million a year, provides an example of how this discourse is deployed. Speaking about the deficit, he said, "the only policy that will work is spending cuts." "Canada has only one choice, only one decision to make" (quoted in *The Toronto Star* 16 September 1994, A1). This same gesture toward political closure is also contained in the federal government's discussion paper *Improving Social Security in Canada*, released in October 1994, which states quite simply that "the status quo is not an option" (Canada 1994b, 8).

According to the neoliberals, the state should neither protect domestic industry from global pressures nor provide a comprehensive social welfare system for its citizens. In effect, this discourse attempts to decentre and displace the Keynesian welfare state with "hyper-liberal" impositional claims about self-regulating market forces and the primacy of the market in generating a new social order (Cox 1991, 342; Drache and Gertler 1991, 7). In the process, it elevates economics over politics and suggests this process is somehow inevitable, neutral, and beyond our control.

> The idea that a country's economic fortunes are largely determined by its success on world markets is a hypothesis, not necessarily truth; and as a practical empirical matter, that hypothesis is flatly wrong. (Krugman 1994, 30)

Of course, this market-driven approach to changes in the global economy is neither inevitable nor neutral. It is a self-interested impositional claim which establishes particular forms of domination and exclusions and, ultimately, must be contested as such. In fact, it is not immediately apparent that the world's economy is globalizing. As Krugman argues, it is "simply not the case that the world's leading nations are to any important degree in economic competition with each other" (Krugman 1994, 30). Moreover, not all countries have adopted a neoliberal strategy and that those which have are not faring particularly well in the new world order.

> A market is a political device to achieve certain outcomes, conferring relative benefits on some and costs on others. . . . It is in essence a political institution that plays a crucial role in structuring society and international politics. (Underhill 1994, 19)

Beyond the question of the wisdom of a market-driven adjustment strategy, however, is its political function. In effect, it is an assault on the logic of the welfare state and the mass-based democracy which has characterized liberal democracies for most of this century. The idea that the market will determine both the direction of economic growth and resource allocation effectively takes these issues off the political agenda. In the process, it silences groups which seek to influence public policy to achieve greater social equity (McBride and Shields 1993, 32). The ascendency of the market thus closes political spaces, demobilizing and excluding those very groups most likely to challenge the growing social inequalities that restructuring is creating (Cox 1994, 50).

It is important to stress that the ascendency of the market over politics does not mean that the state is disappearing. Rather, state power has been redeployed from social welfare concerns and economic management to the enforcement of the market model in virtually all aspects of everyday life. The replacement of the welfare state with a neoliberal alternative very definitely requires political intervention—"the state is to be simultaneously rolled back and rolled forward" (Gamble 1988, 28). It has taken on the job of convincing us that market rationality (itself a questionable term) should take precedence over political negotiation and the collective will of the public (Gill 1992, 178).

International Trading Agreements

Restructuring discourse attempts to depoliticize the market by representing it as natural and self-regulating, and to close off spaces for political negotiation, perhaps most irreversibly through international trading agreements. These agreements are completely saturated with neoliberal assumptions and solutions which serve to erode national sovereignty and limit the ability of governments to respond to the demands of the electorate. Changes in the regulation of international capitalism through GATT and regional treaties such as CUFTA, NAFTA, and the Single European Act effectively represent a "new constitutionalism" which defines and guarantees new rights to transnational capital—rights which often trump those of the citizens of liberal democracies such as Canada (Gill 1992).

Canada's entry into both the CUFTA and the NAFTA was very much an elite driven exercise which, according to one public opinion poll after another, the majority of Canadians did not want. For example, only one month before the Chretien government took Canada into NAFTA in January 1994, a poll showed that fully 63 percent of Canadians were against it (Cohen 1993b). The extent to which these agreements limit Canadian democracy, however, is yet to be fully realized. CUFTA, for example, specifically limits the terrain of the political by prohibiting governments from either favouring domestic producers or subsidizing national industry. NAFTA goes even further by attempting to cap the domain of the state. This document refers to the public sector as "non-conforming" measures, limits the use of public corporations, and requires those remaining to operate according to "proper" commercial operations and considerations such as the profit motive (Cohen 1993b). Moreover, NAFTA imposes new legal restrictions on government regulation of corporations. In effect, governments are denied the ability to take goods and services off the market without having to pay huge compensation costs to business enterprises (Robinson, 1993b, 339).

NAFTA is a profoundly anti-public sector document (Cohen 1993b). It stipulates that all levels of government must declare those things which exclusively rest with the public sector within two years after the implementation of the agreement. Those services not named will be deemed "tradeable" or opened to private sector (transnational) competition and provision. Meanwhile, explicit exclusions such as health care will be reviewed in 1998, the same year that federal funds for medicare are to be phased out in several provinces (Woman to Woman 1993). NAFTA, in other words, attempts to draw a new boundary between the public and private by reducing the public sector and pre-empting any new growth. It sends the clear message that we have reached, indeed surpassed, the appropriate boundary of state intervention in the economy and that restructuring demands retreat and attrition.

The constraints imposed on Canadian governments by international trading agreements obviously hold ominous implications for women and for the achievement of women's equality, as it does for all other subordinate groups. These agreements can dictate how, indeed whether or not, governments can initiate equity-based policies such as, for example, a national daycare program, or protective regulations. Additionally, they transfer important decision-making power to trade tribunals, close spaces of political negotiation, delegitimize non-economic political actors, and elevate market considerations as the prime criteria for determining public policy. For women who have historically been marginalized in Canadian politics and have only recently won a measure of political influence this is a net loss. Increasingly mass democracy becomes an illusion rather than the guiding mechanism for public policy-making and for the creation of social consensus.

RECODING THE PUBLIC AND THE PRIVATE

The forging of the neoliberal state involves a complex redeployment of state power and a displacement of the political terrain once occupied by the welfare state. While the emerging state form maintains all the trappings of sovereignty and executive authority, it, nonetheless, rests on impositional claims which valorize the private over the public (Jessop 1993, 22). Critical governing instruments of the Keynesian welfare state such as public corporations and social welfare programs are said to be "re"-privatized to the market or the home, thereby creating the illusion that they are being returned to some place where they naturally belong. Privatization has been enforced through two other "refunctions"—the recommodification of claims and the reconstitution of domestic enclaves.

Recommodification rests on the unverifiable assertion that services and assets initially created in the public sector for the benefit of all Canadians are better delivered and maintained through market mechanisms and the price system. In the process, they are removed from the realm of political negotiation and subjected to market-oriented rather than political or moral evaluative criteria (Yeatman 1990, 173). In the deceptively simple language of public choice theory, these services and assets are transformed from public goods to private goods. It also means that only those who can muster purchasing power are able to obtain these goods. The reconstitution of the domestic, in contrast, rests on impositional claims about the role and value of the hetero-patriarchal family as a foundation for society. This emphasis on the family is particularly stark in new right rhetoric which blames both the welfare state and feminism for the breakdown of the family and the social fabric. More broadly, however, there is a growing consensus that families should look after their own and that the state should make sure that they do (Abbott and Wallace 1992, 2).

Feminist rhetoric is sometimes appropriated to rationalize the shift of collective responsibility onto individuals in the domestic sphere. Provincial governments have been quick to act on feminist demands to hold "deadbeat dads" accountable through increasingly strict enforcement of child support payments. Similarly, the federal government is stressing the enforcement of child support payments, in its proposed welfare reforms, as a way of getting single mothers off the welfare rolls. The message being conveyed here is that the primary responsibility for the well-being of Canadian children is biological and heteropatriarchal. The defunding of battered women's shelters, the deinstitutionalization of the mentally ill, dramatic declines in the length of hospital stays, and decreasing public support for daycare and elderly care are other examples of this trend. More often, however, the state reconstitutes the domestic by fiat instead of explicit regulation. Privatization and the erosion of the welfare state have the effect of forcing health, child, and elderly care back onto the family and the unpaid work of women. As a result, many women are forced to leave the paid labour force or settle for low-paying part-time employment to meet these caring needs.

Privatization involves much more than simply removing things from the public basket and placing them on the market or in the domestic sphere. The things moved are themselves transformed into something qualitatively different—a lesson we ignore only at a cost. As services and responsibilities are shifted from the public to the private, they become differently encoded, constructed, and regulated. Citizens with a universal right to health care or just plain sick people, for example, become defined as consumers of alternative medical delivery systems who are capable of purchasing choice. Meanwhile, health care providers and treatments are evaluated in terms of cost-effectiveness and marketability. Or, the deinstitutionalized schizophrenic becomes "a street person" and is regulated more often by the police than by mental health professionals. Similarly, the realm of family responsibility is magnified but, at the same time, family relations become subject to increasing surveillance. Governments become central to "regulated self-regulation" in the form of anti-smoking campaigns and other life-style regulations, tax incentives for private retirement savings, or new representations of family relations through concepts such as child, wife, or elder abuse (Jessop 1993, 10). Whether through market-oriented discourse or some other regulatory practice, the underside of "re"-privatization is reregulation, enforced by the state.

HOLLOWING OUT THE WELFARE STATE

A defining mark of the emerging neoliberal state is the "subordination of social policy to the demands of labour market flexibility and structural competitiveness" through the progressive "hollowing out" of the welfare state (Jessop 1993, 9). Restructuring discourse, however, is often less concerned with the actual size of the welfare state than its underlying ideals, especially the idea that everyone is entitled to state protection from unpredictable market forces. In fact, federal spending on social services increased by 42 percent during the Conservatives' second term in office (Spears 1993). Even though the debt is often cited as the rationale for cutting back on social services, the issue is less about budgets than about cultural forms and public expectations (Yeatman 1990, 118, 123). The Mulroney government, for example, declared that it would guard Canada's social welfare system as "a sacred trust," but then fundamentally altered and diminished it through sustained budget cuts. Changing public expectations about entitlements, collective provision for social needs, and the appropriateness of the welfare state has been a critical victory for neoliberalism.

> The next generation of social programs must . . .
> actively create opportunity for Canadians and,
> in so doing, help drive economic growth. (Canada
> 1994b, 9)

During the past decade, the postwar social safety net has been stressed and redesigned almost beyond recognition. This assault began in full force after the re-election of the Mulroney Conservatives in 1988 when they effectively put an end to the principle of universality in welfare provision. Additionally, the Mulroney government unilaterally rewrote the terms of federal-provincial cost-sharing in the fields of social welfare, health care, and post-secondary education. In so doing, it effectively offloaded the fiscal crisis onto the provinces which differ greatly among themselves in their capacity to cope. Most have been forced to decrease services, make entitlements more restrictive, and raise taxes. The combined impacts of the federal transfer cuts to the provinces and the recession have played havoc with the combined provincial debt. In 1989-90, for example, the total provincial debt amounted to $4.7 billion, but it rose to $25 billion only three years later (*The Toronto Star* 24 December 1993, B1). This fiscal imbalance has accelerated the dismantling of welfare services at the provincial level.

The list of social programs which have been reduced or altered by the federal and provincial governments is large and growing daily. These changes, moreover, usually have been implemented "stealth style." This politics, which was perfected by the Mulroney government and subsequently embraced by the federal Liberals and most provincial governments, enables governments to enact immediate and significant changes in social policy by means of complex changes in regulations and repeated budget cuts, without prior public consultation, political mobilization, or media scrutiny (Gray 1990, 382). The politics of stealth was used to put an end to the principle of universality in Canada's Old Age Security and Family Allowance programs and has severely restricted the provinces' capacity to finance social welfare schemes.

Given that women are overrepresented among the ranks of both welfare recipients and state workers, these cuts necessarily have a disproportionately negative effect on them. And, as the research by, among others, Pat Armstrong shows, these negative effects are often felt in the most subtle and personal ways. For example, federal offloading has put severe stress on Canada's health care system and on the women who either work in it or are attended by it. Nurses are being deskilled in a leaner and meaner work environment, people in need of treatment are being deinstitutionalized in ever greater numbers, and the length of hospital stays is dropping dramatically. It is not uncommon for a new mother to be sent home within hours of the delivery of her baby. This would appear to respond to the demands of the women's health care movement that childbirth be de-medicalized and that women be given more control over the birthing process. At the same time, however, these women are being sent home often without sufficient instruction for the care of newborns and without a support system within the home (Armstrong 1995).

The discourse around health care is changing, putting greater emphasis on a woman's private responsibilities for her own health and for caring for the needs of family members. The health care system, in other words, is being incrementally "privatized." Health increasingly is cast in terms of private "life-style" instead of social factors, and the costs of health care are being downloaded to the home and women's unpaid labour. Furthermore, this attack on women is being rationalized precisely with the progressive discourse of the women's health movement. The success of a new order often depends on its ability to incorporate criticisms of the old order, even if the outcomes are qualitatively different. Previous demands by the women's health movement for a de-medicalized and woman-friendly health care model are being used to support health care cuts and to place more responsibility on families and individual women (Armstrong 1995).

The downloading of care work to the private sphere and the unpaid work of women is based on assumptions about the postwar gender order which no longer hold today. The disappearance of the family wage has necessarily pushed most married women into the workforce while the incidence of sole parent families headed by women has mushroomed in recent decades. Thus, as a working paper released by the International Labour Organization in 1993 rightly concludes, women are facing an "intensification of the trade-off between women's producer and non-producer roles" (Baden 1993, 41). Caring work, moreover, becomes invisible and less socially valued with its privatization and decommodification. To the extent that caring work is undervalued with regard to benefits and political respect, women will suffer disproportionately (Orloff 1993, 313).

REDEFINING CITIZENSHIP

It has become increasingly apparent that the new neoliberal state marks a distinct shift in new shared understandings of what it means to be a Canadian citizen and what the citizen can legitimately ask of the state. Although varying considerably among themselves, postwar welfare states rested on a broad but ultimately fragile consensus about the rights of citizenship. The postwar notion of social citizenship conveyed the idea that poverty was not always an individual's fault and that all citizens had the right to a basic standard of living. The general consensus underlying the creation and maintenance of the welfare state was that Canadians should not have to repeat the harsh lessons in public administration dealt out by the Great Depression of the 1930s. The postwar consensus held that the public could enforce limits on the market, that people were not to be forced to engage in market activities which denied their safety or dignity, and that the national community was responsible for the basic well-being of its individual members.

It is precisely this postwar ideal of social citizenship that is currently under attack in the new order. As the Canadian experience demonstrates, there has been a decided shift away from the idea of universal publicly provided services as a right of citizenship. The social safety net is poised for a major transformation to make it fit with the market-based, self-reliant, and privatizing ideals of the new order. The rights and securities guaranteed to all citizens of the Keynesian welfare state are no longer rights, universal, or secure. The new ideal of the common good rests on market-oriented values such as self-reliance, efficiency, and competition. The new good citizen is one that recognizes the limits and liabilities of state provision and embraces her or his obligation to work longer and harder in order to become more self-reliant (Drache 1992, 221). Moreover, as we shall see in the next chapter, there is little tolerance for making "special" claims on the basis of difference or systemic discrimination.

Many of the changes to the social welfare system have occurred incrementally and almost invisibly, usually implemented by cash-strapped provincial governments desperately seeking any way to reduce expenditures by "reforming" social welfare policy. Some governments initially tried to make the poor disappear both literally and conceptually. Alberta, for example, will give welfare recipients a free *one-way* ticket out of the province and keeps payments for so-called "single employables" so low that they are encouraged to seek social assistance elsewhere (*The Toronto Star* 24 December 1993, B1). Similarly, the Mulroney government established a parliamentary sub-committee, which the opposition parties boycotted, to redefine what it meant to be poor in Canada. According to this committee's analysis, Canada's poverty numbers were "grossly exaggerated" and were "hurting Canada's international reputation." It recommended that a new poverty measure be designed—one which would establish the income necessary only to ensure that the poor could meet their most basic needs (*The Toronto Star*, 9 June 1993, A1).

Other provinces, with the encouragement of the federal government, have begun to target welfare populations which have been identified as large drains on the system. Single mothers have been targeted as an immediate problem. Although the childcaring activities of single mothers previously were considered to be of overriding importance, effectively making them unemployable until their children were of school age, this is no longer the current thinking. Public policy is reshaping the social identities of single mothers and their capacity to make claims on the state by redefining them as the welfare problem—as undeserving, employable, and dependent (Evans 1995). For example, New Brunswick, the province that federal Human Resources Minister Lloyd Axworthy calls an "incubator of reform," has launched two programs targeted at single mothers. Axworthy has praised the province for its initiatives in social welfare reform where, he says, "rather than using [social assistance] in a passive way for people to get some limited income security, it gives them a launching pad into the job market" (York 1993). These initiatives, NB WORKS and the Self-Sufficiency Project, attempt to nudge single parents (read women) from the welfare rolls into the job market. More recently, the federal and Manitoba governments have launched a $26.2 million program to help that province's 4,000 single parents currently on welfare to find work (*The Globe and Mail* 10 September 1993, A4). In each case, single mothers are being targeted as "a problem" within the existing welfare system.

All of these provincial initiatives pale in comparison to Ottawa's current "rethinking" of the social welfare system. There has been a great deal of build-up and promotion of the redesigning of the social safety net— a process which essentially puts an end to the postwar social compact. The Chretien government has announced a total redrawing of Canada's social welfare system by 1996—an undertaking that Finance Minister Martin has called "the most comprehensive reform of government policy in decades" (Canada 1994a, 2). On the release of the federal government's discussion paper, *Improving Social Security in Canada* (*ISSC*) in October 1994, the prime minister said that "reforming social security" was on top of the government's legislative agenda. All Canadian women will be affected by these changes in so much as it is aimed at reviewing unemployment and welfare benefits. The forthcoming reforms in Canada's postwar social welfare regime, as well as to fiscal federalism, represent nothing less than a "constitu-(tive)-tional" change in cultural and political understandings.

The new welfare thinking is premised on a human resources model which sees joblessness as an individual rather than structural problem. It is premised on a radical individualism that "locates the causes of social problems in individual failure or misbehaviour and identifies social change as being affected by individuals trying to maximize their personal self-interest" (Williams 1989, 22). This is, at best, an optimistic assumption, especially during what some have termed Canada's "jobless recovery." New Brunswick's Premier McKenna suggests that this type of recovery should not be a concern because "if you have the training, the jobs will take care of themselves" (*The Globe and Mail* 15 January 1993, A1). For the federal government, Canada's mounting social welfare rolls reflect a "skills deficit" which can be reversed by creating a better trained workforce. Critics of the new thinking about "active" social policy are less convinced (McFarland 1993). For many, especially for a generation of young Canadians who have been virtually shut out of the labour force in recent years, the greatest disincentive to employment is not the absence of skills but, quite simply, the absence of jobs!

> Trapping people in dependency is both costly and cruel. (Canada 1994b, 8) Our social programs need to be made more responsible . . . (which) means reforming the system so that it builds bridges to work—to independence, not dependence. (Canada 1994a, 9)

The *ISSC* degenders women, defining them as employable individuals instead of mothers, and then regenders them as welfare dependents in need of therapeutic intervention. In fact, it is hard to find women in this discussion paper even though we know that the provision of social welfare is highly gendered. Some 60 percent of single mothers, for example, live below the poverty line and this group finds strong representation among the ranks of welfare recipients. Under the previous welfare regime, these women were primary seen as mothers but *ISSC* shifts this identity to potential employables. The problem of single parent poverty is no longer a problem. Instead, single mothers are cast as employables—potential workers—who are a burden on the state, their children are the "vulnerable" poor, and "deadbeat dads" become the cause of their poverty.

As the discussion document explains, "one key reason why there is such a close link between poor children and lone-parent families is inadequate, unreliable or unpaid child support payments." The *ISSC* sees the lone-parent family as a degendered one when, in fact, we know the vast majority of these families are female-headed. Putting gender back into the equation might have identified other "key reasons" for child poverty within lone-parent families, such as the poverty of single mothers, the large and persistent wage gap between men and women, marriages broken by male violence against women, ongoing discrimination against lesbians, immigration policies and a persistent racism that hold women of colour at the bottom of the social ladder, the gendered segregation of the labour force, the increased number of women who can only find part-time jobs and, most obviously, the declining availability of affordable, quality childcare in this country.

According to the federal government's new analysis, poverty is very much a problem of skills deficits among individual Canadians who, in turn, become dependent on the social welfare system for survival. The idea that welfare recipients are dependent on welfare carries with it a barrage of negative images which stigmatize the poor and make them appear to be personally to blame for their condition. This rhetorical gesture is not isolated to Canada but is integral to the myths being spun by proponents of the new order. Fraser and Gordon have traced the meaning of dependency through history. They argue that in pre-industrial societies colonies and servants were deemed to be dependent but this did not carry a negative connotation. With industrialization, dependency was assigned to those who were not in the paid labour force. For paupers the term "dependent" implied a weak moral character but for women dependence on the male breadwinner was judged to be natural and proper. Fraser and Gordon argue that in the current period welfare dependency, as with drug addiction, is seen to be an individual shortcoming—one which is both blameworthy and avoidable. All adult "dependency" on the state is now suspect and avoidable. Only children are now able to claim a socially condoned dependence (Fraser and Gordon 1994).

The dependency metaphor also suggests certain policy responses and not others. It raises the spectre of the pathological and dysfunctional and thus invites surgical or technical intervention (Beilhartz 1987). In the case of the federal government's proposals, this involves identifying the diseased/ "the dependents"/the otherwise employable and subjecting them to treatments such as retraining and counselling, creating disincentives to break their habit in the form of workfare, or providing more restrictive and declining benefits. The latter is the rationale underlying the proposed two-tier unemployment insurance system which would pay the so-called "frequent user" (the addict) less than the so-called "occasional user" (the recreational user).

The links between social assistance, dependency, personal culpability, and gender are implicit in the federal government's analysis but the discussion paper goes further. At one point, it suggests that the problem of UI dependency is more pronounced among particular groups, among them, women, members of "visible minorities," persons with disabilities, and Aboriginal people (Canada 1994b, 48). And, at another point, it suggests that single mothers should be helped to "leap successfully from social assistance to the independence of a job—even a low paying one" so that they do not transmit their pathological behaviour to their children. As the discussion paper puts it, "the price of staying on welfare is high . . . children who grow up on society's sidelines risk the continuation of a cycle of low achievement and joblessness" (Canada 1994b, 70). The discussion paper does not question whether low-paying jobs are part of this cycle of poverty.

The *ISSC* fits comfortably into the newspeak of neoliberal governments which attempts to make systemic inequalities invisible and, in the process, silence groups which protest these inequalities. This rhetorical strategy conveys the clear message that it is up to every "good individual" to become more flexible and self-reliant and to make fewer demands on the state. But, a deeply entrenched and unequal gender order, by definition, means that women can only be gendered individuals. As much as this rhetoric tries to cast women as individuals detached from a deeply gendered social order, then, it must necessarily recast them as "bad individuals"—the ones who are different, dependent, and blameworthy for not successfully leaping into independence. Obviously, it is much harder to leap when an individual is burdened by unpaid caring work and gender-based discrimination.

> To continue to pursue social and economic policy as if women do not exist is madness. To have a review of social policy which does not address women's inequality is to throw women to the dogs. (NAC president, Sunera Thobani, *Sunday Star* 2 October 1994, A18)

In *Improving Social Security in Canada*, the federal government sets out its three principal objectives for reforming the social welfare system. These are:

- jobs—helping Canadians to get and keep work by ensuring that they have the knowledge and skills to compete with the best labour forces in the world;
- support of those most vulnerable—providing income support for those in need, while fostering independence, self-confidence, and initiative, and starting to tackle child poverty;
- affordability—making sure the social security system is within the government's means and more efficiently managed, with a real commitment to end waste and abuse (Canada 1994b, 10).

While these objectives seem worthy enough, the suggested mechanisms for their implementation are not. Among other things, the government has put on the table workfare and other penalties for "frequent users" of social welfare and unemployment insurance. Moreover, any increases in welfare spending, the ISSC suggests, should be directed toward counselling rather than income maintenance. The discussion paper states its new understanding of citizenship quite unambiguously. "Improved government support," it suggests, "must be targeted at those who demonstrate a willingness and commitment to self-help." It is the primary task of the reform to make welfare policies more effective by "helping individuals achieve the satisfaction and dignity of work" (Canada 1994b, 25, 82).

> . . . universalism in social policy manufactures its own universal political constituency, which in turn helps maintain a basic sense of social solidarity and shared responsibility. Because universalism grants all members of the citizen body the same rights and treatment, it undermines both the stigmatizing nature of poor relief and . . . the self-reliance mechanism of private insurance. (Esping Anderson 1990, 30)

The disappearance of universal social programs and the erosion of the social safety net obviously reduce the substance of the postwar construction of citizenship. The reform represents a number of foundational shifts in public philosophy and popular thinking. It has reintroduced into politics such notions as the "deserving and undeserving" poor and "genuine" versus "non-genuine" poverty (Yeatman 1990, 122). There is also a shift in thinking about what the reformers refer to as an active welfare model as opposed to the passive outdated postwar one. It is difficult to ignore the obvious valorization of the new order encoded in these terms. They signal a change in the philosophy of welfare provision away from the protection of people who are either temporarily or permanently displaced by the wage economy to a new regime where retraining or participation in the job market is a condition for social assistance. The idea here is that all able-bodied people, very broadly defined without consideration of their social context, are effectively "undeserving" of social assistance if they do not either endeavour to retrain to better compete in the job market, or take some form of work to "top-up" their social assistance incomes, and thus, reduce the burden they impose on the state.

Canada's social welfare system is being redesigned to make it more restrictive, especially for those deemed to be "employable." It aims to force this category back into the job market even if the only jobs available are "non-standard"—i.e., insecure, part-time, poorly paid, and devoid of benefit or union protection (Yeatman 1990, 130). It is no coincidence that these are precisely the kinds of jobs which are being created in Canada's restructured economy. "Active" social welfare programs also serve to rediscipline the workforce both by making the poor dependent on some form of employment to qualify for social assistance, and by constructing an image of the "undeserving" poor as those who do not participate in some way in the job market. All of these factors serve to negate thinking about systemic poverty and unemployment. We are encouraged to think of poverty in terms of undeserving, deficient, and wrongly skilled individuals instead of Canada's "restructured" political economy and its seeming incapacity to provide employment, much less good jobs, for an unacceptable and ever growing number of Canadians. The gaze of government policy-makers is directed away from structural factors (which go unchallenged) and toward the micro-individual self-help solutions. And, it would seem that Canadian women are among those most in need of this kind of therapy. A highly unequal gender order ensures this outcome.

CHAPTER FIVE

The Politics of Marginalization

Since 1984, women's groups have been on the defensive and have struggled hard to maintain the provision of social services as they originally worked to get them. The sense of possibility that characterized the 1970s was replaced with pessimism. (Cohen 1993a, 267)

THE ASCENDENCY OF NEOLIBERAL discourse and the forming of the neoliberal state has put the second wave of the Canadian women's movement on the defensive. Since the election of the federal Progressive Conservatives in 1984, NAC and other women's organizations have been forced to direct ever-increasing quantities of their political currency to defend the welfare state and the principle of gender equality from a multi-faceted neoliberal assault. Women's organizations challenged the so-called "Tory agenda" and were at the forefront of the broad-based political coalitions which opposed the CUFTA, the Meech Lake Accord, the Charlottetown Accord, and the NAFTA. In each case, women's organizations focused on both preserving the rights that women achieved in the Charter of Rights and Freedoms and defending the welfare state.

Women's concerns about the CUFTA initially focused on how the trade deal would impact on women workers, many of whom are immigrant women, in the most vulnerable manufacturing industries such as textiles (Ontario 1987). Soon, however, Women Against Free Trade (WAFT) (which included, among others, representatives of NAC, the Ontario Federation of Labour Women's Committee, the New Democratic Party, and a daycare coalition) issued a manifesto which argued forcefully that much more was at stake for women in the trade deal than simply jobs. It argued that free trade would lower the standard of public services in Canada and diminish the policy-making capacity of Canadian governments (Burstyn and Rebick 1988).

Acutely aware of the trade deal's widespread unpopularity among Canadian voters, the Mulroney government tried to push the CUFTA through Parliament before the critical 1988 federal election. It could then mount a national unity election campaign based on bringing Québec back into Confederation with the Meech Lake Accord. This, however, was not to be. Negotiations with the United States stalled and the Liberal senate dragged its feet, forcing Mulroney to enter the election campaign waving the CUFTA in one hand and the Accord in the other. This was a popular move in Québec, where there appeared to be widespread support for both deals, but it also presented a strategic dilemma for the women's movement. The Meech Lake Accord held the potential to cause a massive rupture between the English and Québécois women's movements. Organizations such as NAC, therefore, made few and cautious pronouncements against the constitutional proposal in order to avoid antagonizing its Québécois counterpart which supported this ultimately futile attempt to draw the province under the umbrella of the Canadian constitution.

Nonetheless, ad hoc women's committees did make presentations outlining their concerns to various provincial inquiries. One consistent thread in their objections was that the process of writing the Meech Lake Accord had been unrepresentative and undemocratic—it was the creation of eleven white men in suits. More tangibly, they argued that the specific provisions of the Accord put women's Charter rights in potential jeopardy, elevating cultural rights over equality rights (Ad Hoc Committee on the Constitution 1988, 143-44).

NAC's most explicit defense of the postwar welfare state came with its unprecedented opposition to the Charlottetown Accord. To the shock of many Canadian women, both inside and outside of the women's movement, as well as its allies within the Canadian labour movement, the NDP, and the reigning political elite, the NAC executive announced in the Fall of 1992 that it would be urging Canadians to vote "NO" in the fast approaching national referendum on the Accord. With this decision, NAC appeared to align itself with some most unlikely allies—the Reform Party and the sovereigntists in Québec. NAC made it clear from the outset, however, that its reasons for not supporting the Accord were fundamentally different from those of the others standing in the "NO" camp. As in the Meech debacle, NAC registered its disdain of the male elite-dominated process which crafted the Accord and of the proposed Canada Clause which potentially could have been used to override women's equality rights guaranteed in Section 15 of the Charter (Day 1993).

The core of NAC's "NO" campaign, however, centred on the Accord's failure to protect universal social programs and to ensure that the federal government maintained its power to establish new ones (Fudge 1993, 8). In particular, NAC was concerned that the Accord would allow the provinces to prevent any future use of federal spending power in areas of provincial jurisdiction. Federal spending power had been the key governing instrument that had created the postwar welfare state and promoted national standards. The women's movement wanted this power to be used again to, among other things, establish a national chidcare program. Speaking on behalf of NAC, then president Judy Rebick argued that "the Charlottetown Accord [would] lead to a dismantling of national social programs and more division and more disunity over the years" (Rebick 1993, 106). In so doing, NAC emerged from the Charlottetown round as one of the few remaining organizational defenders of Canada's postwar welfare regime and of the federal power, although many individual Canadians still support the ideals underlying the postwar welfare state.

This political posture had immediate political consequences. NAC was accused by the governing elite of being part of a self-interested coalition of special-interest groups which "threatened Canadian consensus," indeed were "enemies of Canada" (Fudge 1993, 9). Judy Rebick concluded that the governing elite "responded so viciously to NAC taking a high profile NO position because we were breaking a taboo ... we were taking a strong position on something that wasn't traditionally considered our issue" (quoted in Gottlieb 1993, 382).

> The marginalized could, apparently, comment on an agenda set by the power-holders, but only if our comments were confined within the parameters established by them. If we suggested that the agenda itself was too narrow, that the questions being asked were not the only, or the most pertinent, ones this was considered subversive, violent and essentially undemocratic. (NAC Vice President Shelagh Day on the Charlottetown consultations, Day 1993, 59)

The hostility directed toward women's organizations during the Referendum campaign was only part of a broader concerted attack—some would say a backlash—against feminism and the Canadian women's movement, especially during the Mulroney government's second mandate. At the time, journalists commonly joked that feminism had become the new "F" word on Parliament Hill. Furthermore, the Mulroney administration broke a long-standing tradition of federal officials meeting with NAC annually to discuss their policy concerns and the federal government's progress toward its stated goal of gender equality. It also used deficit reduction rhetoric to justify cuts to its support for NAC and as a means of dismantling some of the women's movement's key strategic resources. Women's centres, women's journals, and the Court Challenges Program, which provided the financial underpinnings for the Legal Education and Action Committee, all fell under the budget's axe.

> The women's movement in Canada is very much based in government funded service organizations and these organizations are struggling to survive, and may not survive, many of them. (Judy Rebick 1994, 62)

It would be a strategic mistake to interpret these cuts merely as a financial "slap on the wrist" wielded by a vindictive federal government, or, for that matter, part of its failed efforts at deficit reduction. The political interventions of the women's movement during the past decade and its repeated collisions with the emerging neoliberal state signal a watershed in the women's movement's postwar identity and politics. Organized groups such as NAC have been forced to shift their public presence from a recognized lobby group with an expectation of access to federal decision-makers to part of a broad-based coalition which is fundamentally opposed to and outside of the emerging neoliberal state. Closed doors to elected officials, funding cuts, the disappearance of women in social policy documents, and the perverse allegation that organized feminists are not part of the democratic polity but, instead, the enemies within—all of these are merely symptoms of the redefinition and displacement of the women's movement as we came to know it in the postwar years.

POLITICS ON THE MARGINS

> The costs of restructuring the economy could be loaded much more easily on to (women and blacks in particular) such groups if the political credibility of their case for equal rights had first been destroyed. (Gamble 1988, 16)

As Gamble argues about Thatcherism, a key component of the politics of restructuring has been a sustained attack on equality-seeking groups, especially the women's movement. Comparative experiences suggest that restructuring discourse attempts to marginalize and unravel emancipatory movements in at least two critical ways. One form of marginalization is to deny the movement's social significance, making it appear instead as a sectoral and self-interested lobby group. The other form is to constitute particular members of the women's movement as lying on the outer limits of the norm—outside of the ordinary. They are recast as pathological individuals or disadvantaged groups for whom special provision and intervention is necessary in order to make them ordinary (Yeatman 1990, 130).

"Special Interests" and the Neoliberal State

These marginalizing moves are clearly evident in the Canadian experience. At worst, feminists have been accused of not representing the core of Canadian women but, instead, a radical fringe of man-haters, lesbians, and leftists determined to undermine the family and traditional values. More broadly, it is argued that feminist organizations such as NAC do not represent the mainstream of Canadian women. This sentiment was first expressed by REAL (Realistic, Equal, and Active for Life) Women in their repeated attempts to gain federal funding made available for groups that "promote the advancement of women." The federal Conservatives judged that REAL Women met this standard even though the organization actively opposes equal-pay-for-work-of-equal-value, reproductive choice, and greater constitutional protection for women's rights. Later, Conservative leadership candidate Kim Campbell vowed that, when she became prime minister, she would stop giving money to "advocacy groups" such as NAC, arguing that they should be funded by their private constituencies (*The Globe and Mail* 13 June 1993, A6). This sentiment was revisited in the federal Liberal government's first budget of 22 February 1994 which reduced all group funding by 5 percent. Finance Minister Martin also promised to consider whether the federal government should get out of the business of funding "lobby groups" altogether.

The idea that the women's movement is a self-interested lobby group has been a central theme in the rhetoric of the Reform Party and its leader Preston Manning. There are a raft of groups which Reform spokespersons decry as being "special interests" and, as such, threats to representational democracy in Canada. These include, among others, the women's movement, native organizations, organized labour, and multicultural, linguistic, and ethnic groups (Laycock 1994, 217). It is the Reform's position that these groups, aligned with an unaccountable and power-hungry federal bureaucracy, form a "tyranny of minorities" over the majority of Canadians. The Reform Party argues that the federal government should stop both funding "special interest" groups and giving them privileged access to the state. As a 1992 Reform pamphlet argues, "in Ottawa, every special interest group counts except one: Canadians" (quoted in Laycock 1994, 219).

More recently, the attack on so-called "special interests" has moved to the Liberal government's backbenches. In November 1994, for example, Hamilton-Wentworth Member of Parliament John Bryden released a report calling for the establishment of a parliamentary committee to examine "the financial aspects and implications of Canada's charity and non-profit industries," as well as the end of government funding for those groups "whose primary special interest is lobbying, advocacy, or the promotion of a special agenda or viewpoint" (Bryden 1994, 4). According to the Bryden report, "ordinary" Canadians disagree with the idea of government funding groups that exist primarily for their own self-interest, or to push their own political agenda (ibid., 10).

But who are in these special interest groups? The Bryden report gives us a key to identifying the "self-interested":

> The buzz words identifying these groups are "lobbying," "advocacy," "promotion," and "education." When these words are encountered in the literature of a not-for-profit organization, they signal one category of "special interest group" as ordinary people understand the term. . . . Another measure of "special interest" is exclusivity ... [groups that] define themselves in terms of members of the same faith, cultural background, language, economic, ethic and so on. The special interest involves who people are rather than what they do. (ibid., 9-10)

Although the women's movement is broad-based, inclusive, and emancipatory, restructuring discourse attempts to label it and other new social movements as "special" and, by implication, unrepresentative. Why, we should ask, is it not in the common interest of all to promote, educate, and advocate for the equality of the majority of Canadians who are women? Additionally, restructuring discourse attempts to cast social movements which seek to empower the marginalized as threats to democracy itself. It is argued that they threaten to "hijack the political agenda" and disrupt the political process (Phillips 1992, 6). Barbara McDougall, a former minister in the Mulroney cabinet, suggested the current problem of governing Canada is that "so many single or limited interest groups have established their presence on the national political scene that it is virtually impossible for any government to undertake a comprehensive policy platform" (quoted in Phillips 1993, 12). For Preston Manning, the fear is that "feminist extremists" will "hijack the women's movement and discredit it from the rest of the population" (quoted in Sigurdson 1994, 268). Manning has denied that statements such as these are, in any sense, anti-woman. As he writes in his book, *The New Canada*, the Reform Party is a "potential political home for women with traditional values and for those who want more fairness in male-female relationships," but "not for those who carry these values and concerns to extremes" (Manning 1992, 354).

The Ordinary Canadian

The terrorist imagery underlying these statements is readily apparent. The women's movement is represented as made up of fringe groups, extremists, and hijackers in order to delegitimize it in the public eye. This imagery is further reinforced by contrasting social movements with the favourite son of the emerging order—"the ordinary Canadian." This is not his first incarnation in Canadian politics. The NDP raised his spectre in the 1970s in order to emphasize its support for "ordinary working people" as opposed to faceless corporations (Brodie and Jenson 1988, 309). The current juxtaposition between the "ordinary Canadian" and "special interests," however, evokes a very different and disturbing politics. For one thing, profit organizations (corporations) are not cast as "special" with interests antagonistic to the ordinary Canadian, or as having their own agenda, or as promoting their own point of view. For another, the designation of the women's movement as a "special interest group" implies that its demands are not in the general interest. "Special interest groups" do not speak for the ordinary Canadian but, instead, demand privileges which are unearned and violate the new norms of citizenship. Similarly, defining "special" needs groups and targeting them for intensive state intervention casts them outside the community of ordinary citizens who presumably are able to attend to their own needs.

The neoliberal's "ordinary Canadian" has appeared only recently on the Canadian political stage. He figures prominently in the rhetoric of the Reform Party. This party has skilfully and repeatedly evoked the supposed opposition between the ordinary and the special Canadian. According to Manning, policies such as bilingualism and multiculturalism have created conditions of special status which are incompatible with citizen equality— an unhyphenated Canadianism. The ordinary Canadian was also hailed by the Spicer Commission, which was established to gather public opinion on constitutional reform, as the source of Canadian values. It was later revealed, however, that Spicer's ordinary Canadians were a very hand-picked lot (Campbell and Pal 1994). The ordinary Canadian was also invited to the Mulroney government's series of constitutional meetings which were quickly organized before the referendum on the Charlottetown Accord in order to make the process appear more democratic. Again, most of the delegates invited to these forums carried credentials and affiliations which betrayed any notion that they were drawn from "mainstreet" Canada. The ordinary Canadian also became a media star, becoming a regular on the CBC's 1993 "townhall meetings" election coverage.

But, the ordinary Canadian's role in neoliberal politics does not end here. He was cast as the star, in fact, the only one invited to the federal Liberal's pre-budget consultation meetings that were held in five cities in early 1994. These ordinary Canadians were fed documents which rendered a very limited interpretation of the options available to the federal government; those organizational spokespersons most likely to contest these documents were excluded from the process. NAC president, Sunera Thobani, for example, was not invited to the Toronto budget consultation because she was too high profile—too visible—unlike the faceless Bay Street suits who support the neoliberal agenda. According to one insider, the reason why participation at the pre-budget consultations was so tightly controlled was that the government feared that its agenda would be "hijacked" by oppositional forces as appeared to be the case during the Charlottetown Accord conferences.

Although the ordinary Canadian is increasingly evoked in political rhetoric, his identity is elusive, defined primarily by the things he is not. The ordinary Canadian is disinterested, neither seeking special status nor treatment from the state. He is neither raced, nor sexed, nor classed: he transcends difference. So who is he? A close reading of the current conception of the ordinary Canadian reveals that he can only be a white, heterosexual, middle-class, English-speaking male because, in contrast to him, everyone else is "special" in some way or another (Patten 1994). How then do we interpret the ordinary Canadian's rapid ascendency to the centre of the political stage—a stage which the political elite suggests is congested with special interests which threaten to hijack the political agenda and pervert representational democracy (Leger and Rebick 1993, 95)?

Clearly, the "ordinary Canadian" is a metaphor for something. None of us is ordinary or, put differently, all of us are special in some way or another. So what does it mean for us to defer to the voice of the mythic ordinary Canadian? For one thing, this dichotomy between the "ordinary" and the "special" sends the clear message that regular people do not require state assistance and protection. For another, it tells us that it is no longer legitimate to organize against systemic discrimination. As Iris Marion Young suggests, "contemporary politics increasingly grants political legitimacy to persons on the condition that they do not claim special rights or needs, or call attention to their particular history or culture" (Young 1990, 109). This discursive move effectively reinforces privilege by attempting to silence those who are deemed to be different.

> In a society where some groups are privileged while others are oppressed, insisting that as citizens persons should leave behind their particular affiliations and experiences to adopt a general

> point of view serves only to reinforce that privilege.
> (Young 1989, 257)

The imposed dichotomy between the ordinary and special serves to delegitimize and silence all those who declare themselves to be different, marginalized, and structurally or historically disadvantaged. This new politics obviously is a threat to the women's movement as well as to all other groups, such as people of colour, who suffer from systemic discrimination in Canadian society. As important, this artificial distinction provides the cultural foundations for the changes in citizenship and social welfare entitlement discussed in the previous chapter.

Targeting

> ... the attempt to construct "citizen" identities is one of the important tasks of democratic politics.
> ... The way we define citizenship is intimately linked to the kind of society and political community we want. (Mouffe 1993, 60)

A central theme in the work of Michel Foucault is the idea that how cultures define the normal or ordinary as opposed to the deviant or special both gives people their social and personal identity and acts as an instrument of political domination and bureaucratic administration (Foucault 1973). Restructuring discourse has increasingly employed these "dividing practices" to minimize the relevance of gender in the new cultural order—an impositional claim that attempts to delegitimize the women's movement. Increasingly, the social category, "woman," which found some unity, however misleading, in the welfare state and second-wave feminist discourse, is actively being deconstructed. Women, it is argued, do not have similar political interests. At the same time, individual women are being redefined as members of specially disadvantaged groups which require "targeted" social programs to address their special needs/shortcomings so that they too can become ordinary "degendered" citizens (Yeatman 1990, 134).

The idea of targeting is entirely consistent with the hollowing out of the welfare state. Its overt rationale is that, in an era of fiscal restraint, scarce resources are best targeted at those who need them the most. Thus, universal entitlements such as family allowance are transformed into a child tax credit available only to those whom the government defines as truly needy. Similarly, initiatives designed to combat violence against women are structured to target what are deemed to be high risk groups—Aboriginal women, women of colour, immigrant women, lesbians, and women with disabilities.

Women's different experiences of oppression cannot be denied or ignored. But, responsiveness to difference is not the primary outcome of targeting. Instead of exposing the structural links among race, gender, sexuality, poverty, and violence, targeting serves to pathologize and individualize difference as well as to place the designated groups under increased state surveillance and administrative control. It disassembles and diffuses the collective claims of the women's movement, recasting it as a "ghetto of disadvantaged groups" (Yeatman 1990). The women's movement, as an historical-moral-political concept, with an evolving vision of political inclusion and equality, is deconstructed into a series of disconnected statistical and administrative categories which require some sort of therapeutic intervention to produce self-sufficient individuals.

TOWARD A FEMINIST POLITICS OF RESTRUCTURING

> The abandonment of the discourse of citizenship by dominant groups at this point of time is (neoliberalism's) response to the increasing effectiveness of claims on citizenship by groups historically identified as "other" or, in contemporary parlance, "minorities." (Yeatman 1994, 83)

Although restructuring discourse attempts to draw women into the public either as non-citizens with special needs or as genderless citizens, the restructuring process is, needless to say, neither gender- nor class- nor race-neutral. Indeed, its effects are already painfully obvious in the everyday lives of most Canadian women. The postwar world of a stable nuclear working middle-class family—with a single male provider, where families could save and "get ahead," and mom stayed at home—has disappeared. Full-time jobs are increasingly being replaced with part-time precarious employment, while the number of paid hours required to support an average Canadian household has almost doubled in the past twenty years (NAC, 1992). The vast majority of Canadian women work, albeit often in poorly paid jobs, and the number of female-headed families living in poverty grows annually. Statistics Canada, in fact, reports that family incomes have suffered "their steepest and longest slide in 40 years, pushing record numbers of children into poverty and leaving the average family worse off than it was in 1980," itself a recession year (*The Toronto Star* 22 December 1994, A3).

At the same time, the state has backed away from supporting women workers and their families. Cutbacks in employment and pay equity, education, and retraining programs are threatening to reverse many of the gains that women have made in the past twenty years. This is especially so for immigrant women who have been disproportionately affected by the collapse of the textile and manufacturing sectors since the implementation of CUFTA. Furthermore, cutbacks in social welfare are forcing many women back into the house to provide unpaid care for other family members who are sick, young, old, or disabled. Again, these trends have not gone unnoticed by Ottawa mandarins even though they present their case in a deceptively gender-neutral voice. A recently released study by Statistics Canada entitled "Dimensions of Job-Family Tension" reports that nine out of ten working parents, who have to arrange childcare, experience some tension in juggling job and family responsibilities. For almost one in five that tension is 'severe.' Moreover, the report predicts that job-family stress is likely to increase as working parents are faced with the additional load of caring for elderly relatives as the population ages and alternative and affordable forms of elderly care disappear (*The Toronto Star* 23 December 1994, A1).

Restructuring has disadvantaged most women on both sides of the public/private divide leading some to argue that the emerging new order can only result in a crisis in the provision of basic social needs. Reprivatization, it is argued, depends on the continuing functioning of the patriarchal nuclear family and, indeed, everywhere we see cultural markings which valorize this "ideal family form" (Ursel 1992, 295). The new gender order may be inherently unstable both because this family form is no longer dominant or even viable, and because it anticipates an increase in women's labour both in the market and in the home (Brodie 1994; Fraser 1989; McDowell 1991; Ursel 1992). It would be a mistake, however, to argue that the current redrawing of the public/private divide is doomed to failure merely because the state can no longer enforce the male-headed nuclear family form. Instead, restructuring entails a "restating" of the family form and the domain of the private.

By way of example, the Ontario Law Reform Commission recently recommended that the government recognize "the diversity of family forms" by requiring common law and same sex couples to register with the province. Under this plan, these non-conforming couples would be given all the rights and obligations of married heterosexual couples including support, property, and possession rights (*The Globe and Mail* 18 November 1993, A1). There is nothing inherent in the logic of reprivatization that requires a legally married heterosexual woman to be a home caregiver: a common law spouse, a gay partner, or a single mother can also assume the role.

In other cases, homemaking functions have simply been commodified allowing some women to buy cleaning or caring work from other women, especially from poor women, immigrant women, and women of colour. Intercede, an organization for domestic workers, for example, has reported that in Canada the demand for domestic workers, especially for live-ins who are effectively available to their employers all of the time, now far exceeds supply (Gabriel and Macdonald 1993). The trend toward commodifying domestic labour has been growing in recent years, but reprivatization suggests further intensification and racialization of this process. The new gender order, in other words, carries many contradictions and potential lines of conflict among women themselves but it is not doomed to self-destruct. It does not necessarily require the maintenance of the patriarchal family but, instead, will encode and regulate different family forms and the provision of care-giving. Families, in other words, are part of the complex matrix that shifts and transforms during periods of fundamental restructuring.

Feminism and Neoliberalism

Haraway has argued that the present era is premised on a fundamental paradox—the simultaneous intensification and erosion of gender both literally and metaphorically. Privatization puts renewed emphasis on the so-called feminine sphere of the home and the feminine qualities of selflessness, nurturing, and care-giving. Meanwhile, paid work itself is said to be increasingly "feminized." Stable full-time, high paying jobs are rapidly being replaced by part-time and precarious employment—the kind of work that marked the gendered division of labour and political power in the postwar years. When work is feminized, it is extremely vulnerable. It can easily be drawn into or pushed out of the paid labour force. As well, workers are seen less as workers than as servers. While women and people of colour are all too familiar with this kind of work, what is different about the current era is that often these are the only jobs available for the previously privileged workers of the postwar order—white men (Haraway 1991, 166-68).

> The interests of low-paid workers of both sexes are therefore likely to draw closer together, while it may be increasingly difficult to create a unity of "all women," although there will continue to be areas such as health care and violence where their interests are more likely to coincide. (Wilson 1988, 199)

Increasing evidence of the feminization of work as well as growing racial and class-based disparities among women themselves has lead some feminists to argue that gender is an eroding base for political organizing. In a sense, gender is everywhere and nowhere as McDowell suggests when she writes, "perhaps we are all becoming women workers regardless of biological sex" (McDowell 1991, 418). More explicitly, British socialist feminist

Elizabeth Wilson argues that this sea change demands a recentring of class-based political action. Women should turn from feminist organizing and regroup within the trade union movement alongside working class men. As a result of restructuring, Wilson argues, the interests of low-paid workers of both sexes are drawing closer together. The vulnerable position of the vast majority of women in the labour force should be reason enough for them to support trade unionism (Wilson 1988, 199).

It is one thing to argue that we can no longer assume that all women share the same gender-determined set of political interests, if we ever could. It is quite another thing to suggest that evidence of difference among women disrupts the feminist project. Women have always been divided by class, race, and sexuality to name a few axes of social inequality, of domination, and of subordination. Does recognizing the importance of these divisions, and the power relations that they support, require women to prioritize their class position over their gender or race and reorganize on that basis? The rationale for this argument is not immediately obvious.

Wilson's analysis of the politics of the present conjuncture, I believe, fails to come to terms with both the gendered nature of the trade union movement and the current crisis of the traditional left itself. Historically, women have had a very mixed experience within the trade union movement, often struggling to have gender issues even recognized. Admittedly, the trade union movement has taken important steps to incorporate gender inequalities in its strategic agenda in recent years. Nevertheless, trade unionism is unlikely to be able to address the gendered issues arising from the domestic sphere. This sphere remains a crucial and inequitable site of struggle for most women and this struggle only promises to intensify with the erosion of the welfare state and the privatization of care.

Furthermore, trade unionism and the traditional left also have been pushed into crisis by the emerging neoliberal order. The collapse of the Soviet Union, the disappearance of assembly-line production in western countries, declining rates of unionization, the proliferation of part-time employment, the growth of self-employment, home work and small workplaces, the increasing individualization and commodification of public goods, and the challenge of new social movements have largely debilitated the traditional left in recent years (Mouffe 1993, 9). The number of unionized workers has plunged, leaving the trade union movement as a declining base from which to launch opposition to the new order. Moreover, like second-wave feminism, the traditional left was totally unprepared for restructuring and neoliberalism's attack on the welfare state and, to this point, it has been unable to provide a coherent alternative to the emerging new order. Nostalgia for the good old days of the welfare state and trade union power, with the associated costs of denying gender (and racial) oppression, can only ensure the traditional left's continued decline.

Fundamentally, Wilson assumes that women must embrace one shared identity, that of worker, in order to be legitimate political actors. This fixation on a singular identity, one form of social inequality, however, is precisely the reason why the traditional left has been unable to amass a coherent alternative to neoliberalism. The traditional left's conception of a more fundamental and morally superior politics which revolves around a (male) class-identified revolutionary subject simply does not fit with the political terrain. It is populated by a much more complex array of oppositional forces, among them feminists, environmentalists, Native peoples, and anti-racist groups (Haraway 1991, 176). Indeed, the current crisis of the traditional left and trade unions may be attributed precisely to the fact that these political actors have been largely impervious to these new political actors with distinct claims on the political. These new political actors do not accept the proposition that all oppression is ultimately reducible to their class position, nor should they.

I am not arguing that feminists should avoid struggling alongside and within the labour movement against the many injustices of the emerging neoliberal order. A feminist politics of restructuring necessarily entails broad-based alliances across gender, race, and class. As Haraway puts it, the new order makes "cross-gender and race alliances on issues of life support necessary, not just nice" (Haraway 1991, 168). But the foundations for these coalitions defy a prior determination. The current politics of uncertainty demands a recognition of contradictory and multiple identities, some of which will assume political primacy at certain times and with respect to certain issues. Both in the past and especially now, political coalitions are neither natural, nor obvious, nor dictated by political theories carved out of a different world. They have to be constructed and maintained within the context of particular times and cultures (Pringle and Watson 1992, 66).

> What we have to recognize is that there is a new reality taking shape. . . . This has profound implications for political strategy. (Magnussen and Walker 1988, 55)

The question of identity and coalition is intimately tied to that of the "where" of a feminist politics of restructuring. As earlier chapters describe, the emergence of the neoliberal state has closed many political spaces for marginalized groups while international trading agreements have served to limit the capacities of national governments to respond to the electorate. This has lead some to argue that feminists should by-pass the national state and focus instead on the global. The globalization of capital, it is argued, requires a similar global organization of the women's movement. This sentiment is sometimes expressed with the phrase "The Sisterhood is Global," but there are a number of reasons why feminists should be wary of this kind of rhetoric. For one thing, the idea rests on universalizing and homogenizing assumptions which ignore the very real and different stakes that women, especially in the North and the South, have in the restructuring process (Gabriel and Macdonald 1993). While making appeals to the "Global Sisterhood" is an important strategic and political device, we should never assume that all of the oppressive strands of restructuring always "add up in the same direction." If the debates within feminism have taught us anything, it is that there is no single or universal "woman." This, and the realization that western women can be, at one and the same time, both the victims and beneficiaries of globalization, has forced western mainstream feminism to "lose its innocence" (Yeatman 1993, 228). It has lost the moral highground that comes with the depiction of all women everywhere as victims of partriarchy. A feminist politics necessarily has become one of "negotiating a path between always impure positions" (Grosz 1990, 342).

Some feminist theorists see the disappearance of the myth of a "womanly unity" as the end of the women's movement, but others argue that this is not a "cause for mourning" or for the disappearance of a feminist politics (Gordon 1991, 103). Mouffe, for example, contends that the new feminist politics depends on rejecting essentialist identities. Feminist politics, after all, is not simply about women. It is about emancipation, representation, democracy, and equality. And, these goals must always be pursued "within a wider articulation of demands" arising from the multiple axes of oppression which operate within the new order (Mouffe 1993, 87).

The problems which arise from the idea of a global feminist movement, however, do not revolve around identity alone. There is also the issue of sites of struggle. Although it is clear that the terrain of politics has shifted, it is less obvious that it has shifted away from the nation state to some stateless global space. For one thing, those arguing for a globalization of oppositional politics may misdiagnose the problem when they accept this depiction of the new order. Restructuring discourse stresses the necessity and inevitability of globalized production and a borderless world but this is not the world, in fact, that restructuring has created to this point. Instead, there have been a variety of different state responses to the changing international order, a central one being the formation of highly protectionist regional trading blocs such as the North American trading bloc and a single Europe. In other words, the global metaphor may be inappropriate. If there is to be a supranational feminist politics, it may be more effective to forge coalitions within trading blocs than across them.

Another problem with the global solution is that it implicitly accepts the neoliberal impositional claim that the ability of the national state to respond to democratic impulses has disappeared. This claim obviously directs our political energies away from the national state and obscures the fact that the state has been fully implicated in the process of globalization (Panitch 1993, 35). It thus serves to depoliticize political actors and social movements by suggesting that the political playing field has ascended to an abstract global space that they cannot immediately access, much less identify.

CONCLUSION

So to borrow a question which should always elude a permanent answer: what is to be done? No single answer will suffice because ultimately the political objectives, indeed, the very survival of the women's movement under the neoliberal state depends on the collective decisions and strategies. The purpose of this book has been to begin a debate about where the Canadian women's movement finds itself at the end of the twentieth century and about where it wants to go. I have tried to argue that social movements are part of the complex matrix of cultural forms which are transformed during an era of restructuring. Oppositional movements that ignore or deny the shifting political terrain or that fail to explore their own historical origins and potential for transformation are destined to become part of the history that they cling to.

In many ways, the question of "where" to focus feminist politics in an era of restructuring—at the global, the national, or the local level—begs a much more fundamental question about the political itself. Mouffe, for example, argues that "it is indeed the political which is at stake here, and the possibility of its elimination" (Mouffe 1993, 1). I have attempted to show that the passing of the welfare state has displaced many of the sites and objects of political struggle for the Canadian women's movement and that this transformation has been enacted throughout the social structure through neoliberal impositional claims. It is at this level—of contesting the neoliberal orthodoxy—where a feminist politics of restructuring must begin.

For the most part, Canadians have been too quick to accept the determinism and unrestrained economism of restructuring discourse. We have not sufficiently challenged its impositional claims as "impositional"—as invested interpretations of reality which favour certain groups over others. These impositional claims should be subjected to political contestation and moral evaluation. We are living through a period of profound adjustment. On this we can all agree. But it is an impositional claim to suggest that this adjustment *must* occur on the terrain of gender and of social policy, and to suggest that societies must restructure according to market criteria. Our silence has implicitly endorsed neoliberalism's capacity to delegitimize political, cultural, and moral claims (Yeatman 1990, 102). The current feminist project must be one of "recovering the political" (Benhabib 1993, 111).

> We can either fatalistically accept this removal of economic policy from the control of democratic institutions and face economic and social erosion or we can fight back and defend our right to strengthen democratic controls over economic life. (Grinspun and Kreklewich 1994, 34)

In many ways, the Canadian women's movement has already begun to take the lead in interrogating restructuring discourse and the social relations it underwrites. For one thing, it has challenged the idea that market-driven development need not be held accountable for its impact on women. Although the discourse on globalization is largely illusory, there are international political spaces that attempt to hold governments accountable for human rights, for gender equality, and for the protection of women workers. NAC, among others, has begun the difficult but important task of linking the gendered underpinnings of restructuring and the neoliberal state with the protection of women's human rights. In the months leading up to the Beijing Conference, women's organizations, nationally and internationally, have begun to argue that the new order does not comply with existing international conventions on human rights with which countries such as Canada have agreed to comply. These include, among others, the International Convention on Economic, Social, and Cultural Rights and the Convention on the Elimination of All Forms of Discrimination Against Women, as well as numerous other international codes provided by the United Nations and the International Organization of Labour. As women's organizations contend, economic policies which make women less economically and socially secure, and contribute to women's vulnerability to social and sexual coercion and to violence, are quite simply violations of their human rights and must be contested as such (ECE, 1994). As NAFTA expands its shadow over the western hemisphere, a feminist politics of restructuring should ensure that new trading agreements respect the letter of these conventions and that national governments be held accountable. This strategy provides a basis for coalitions both internally and internationally without assuming a unity of interests.

> Life is not gender neutral and neither are government decisions. (Glenda Simms, president, Canadian Advisory Council on the Status of Women)

81

Equally important, the women's movement is attempting to write gender and systemic discrimination back into the neoliberal state's analysis of Canadian society. No matter how often new public policy initiatives attempt to cast women as genderless "individuals" or as "people," or as "(extra-) ordinary Canadians," the fact remains that women are gendered individuals embedded in a highly and increasingly unequal gender order. Restructuring has brought many changes for Canadian women but also many continuities. The majority of women workers are still trapped in female job ghettos. Men on average still earn much more than women. The economic gulf between women of colour and white women is becoming even more firmly entrenched. Women continue to take primary responsibility for family and community life. And, governments consistently ignore the significant contribution women's unpaid work makes to the economy and society (ECE, 1994, 2).

All of these factors make neoliberalism's depiction of social policy reform as a matter of remedying skills-deficits or of countering individual dependency-pathologies a dangerous misrepresentation of the real problems that Canadian women confront in the mid-1990s. NAC and other women's organizations have been quick to bring gender back into the social policy review process. In a brief presented to federal Minister of Human Resources Development Axworthy in December 1994, Sunera Thobani argued that the reform proposals threaten women on a number of fronts. For example, they completely discount the value of parenting. Is it to the benefit of either Canadian children or society to take single mothers from their children and force them into workfare and training programs? Moreover, can one really separate the issue of child poverty from the feminization of poverty (National Women's Consultation on the Social Security Review, 1994, 2)? Women's groups also question the supposed gender-neutrality of the proposed two-tier unemployment insurance plan. Women necessarily are "frequent" users both because they tend to move in and out of the workforce to have and raise their children or attend to other family members, and because their jobs tend to be more precarious. Canadians should question whether these are valid reasons for locking these women into a lower UI payment schedule. The issues raised by the social reform process are ultimately about social values. As much as federal policy-makers would like to tie the debate about reform to dubious efficiencies and a blind faith in market forces, these values must be measured against equality, fairness, and justice. This is obviously a difficult task when the full force of the state and the media are transmitting the neoliberal ethos into our livingrooms on a daily basis, but it is, nonetheless, a primary task.

The current era provides the women's movement with a fundamental challenge—to interrogate restructuring discourse and to understand the new cultural and political forms that it underwrites. Feminists must learn how to read the webs of power created by restructuring in order to understand the political potential of new coalitions (Haraway 1991 170). This is fundamental because ultimately political spaces open up in relation to existing systems of governance and existing systems of domination. If there is a constant in the politics of liberal democracies it is that political struggle will always erupt around ethical/moral concerns about equality, however it is defined during an historical period (Yeatman 1994, ix). No matter how the dominant political discourse attempts to constrain the political and empower the amoral market forces, the issue of equality will and must fuel a feminist politics of restructuring. And, ultimately, this is how political spaces are opened and how the political is recovered. The women's movement is uniquely placed to begin to forge new coalitions aimed at the long process of reclaiming the public and recovering the political. In a very real sense, the women's movement must begin to "re-public-ize" political spaces and help build a new social consensus about the boundaries and content of the public and private. We are not only responsible for these boundaries: "we are they" (Haraway 1991, 180).

Select Bibliography

Abbott, Pamela, and Claire Wallace. (1992). *The Family and the New Right*. Boulder: Pluto Press.

Abele, Francis. (1992). "The Politics of Competition." In Francis Abele, ed., *How Ottawa Spends 1992-93*. Ottawa: Carleton University Press.

Adamson, Nancy, Linda Briskin, and Margaret McPhail. (1988). *Feminists Organizing for Change*. Toronto: Oxford.

Ad Hoc Committee on the Constitution. (1988). "We Can Afford a Better Accord: The Meech Lake Accord. *Resources for Feminist Research* 17: 3.

Allen, Judith. (1990). "Does Feminism Need a Theory of the State?" In Sophie Watson, ed., *Playing the State: Australian Feminist Interventions*. London: Verso Books.

Althusser, Louis. (1971). *Lenin and Philosophy and Other Essays*. London: New Left Books.

Andrew, Caroline. (1984). "Women and the Welfare State." *Canadian Journal of Political Science* 27: 4 (December).

Armstrong, Pat. (1995). "Unraveling the Social Safety Net." In Janine Brodie, ed., *Women and Canadian Public Policy*. Toronto: Harcourt, Brace and Company.

Backhouse, Constance, and David Flaherty, eds. (1992). *Changing Times: The Women's Movement in Canada and the United States*. Montréal: McGill-Queen's University Press.

Baden, Sally. (1993). *Equality for Women in Employment: An Interdepartmental Project*. Geneva: International Labour Organization.

Bakker, Isabella. (1991). "Pay Equity and Economic Restructuring: The Polarization of Policy." In Judy Fudge and Patricia McDermott, eds., *Just Wages: A Feminist Assessment of Pay Equity*. Toronto: University of Toronto Press.

———— ed. (1994). *The Strategic Silence: Gender and Economic Policy*. London: Zed Books.

————, ed. (1995). *Changing Spaces: Gender and State Responses to Restructuring in Canada.* Toronto: University of Toronto Press.

Begin, Monique. (1992). "The Royal Commission on the Status of Women in Canada: Twenty Years Later." In Constance Backhouse and David Flaherty, eds., *Changing Times: The Women's Movement in Canada and the United States.* Montréal: McGill-Queen's University Press.

Beilhartz, Peter. (1987). "Reading Politics: Social Theory and Social Policy." *Anzjs* 23: 3 (November).

Benhabib, Seyla. (1993). "Feminist Theory and Hannah Arendt's Concept of Public Space." *History of Human Sciences* 6: 2.

Bowles, Samuel, and Hebert Gintis. (1986). *Democracy and Capitalism.* London: Routledge and Kegan Paul.

Boyer, Robert and Daniel Drache, eds. (1995). *Do Nation-States Have A Future?* Montréal: McGill-Queen's University Press.

Brodie, Janine. (1985). *Women and Politics in Canada.* Toronto: McGraw-Hill Ryerson.

————. (1990). *The Political Economy of Canadian Regionalism.* Toronto: Harcourt, Brace, Jovanovich.

————. (1994). "Shifting Public Spaces: A Reconsideration of Women and the State in the Era of Global Restructuring." In Isabella Bakker, ed., *The Strategic Silence: Gender and Economic Policy.* London: Zed Books.

————, ed. (1995). *Women and Canadian Public Policy.* Toronto: Harcourt, Brace and Company.

————, and Jane Jenson. (1988). *Crisis, Challenge and Change: Party and Class in Canada Revisited.* Ottawa: Carleton University Press.

————, and Jane Jenson. (1995). "Piercing the Smokescreen: Stability and Change in Brokerage Politics." In Alain Gagnon and Brian Tanguay, eds., *Canadian Parties in Transition: Discourse, Organization and Representation.* Toronto: Nelson.

————, and Leah Vosko. (1994). "The De-re-gendering of Social Policy." *Canada Watch* 3: 3 (December).

Brown, Wendy. (1992). "Finding the Man in the State." *Feminist Studies* 18: 1 (Spring).

Bryden, John. (1994). "Special Interest Group Funding." Member of Parliament's Report, Ottawa: House of Commons, November.

Burt, Sandra. (1986). "Women's Issues and the Women's Movement in Canada Since 1970." In Alan Cairns and Cynthia Williams, eds., *The Politics of Gender, Ethnicity and Language in Canada.* Toronto: University of Toronto Press.

————. (1994). "The Women's Movement: Working to Transform Public Life." In James Bickerton and Alain Gagnon, eds., *Canadian Politics.*

Second edition. Peterborough: Broadview.

Burstyn, Vardo, and Judy Rebick. (1988). "How 'Women Against Free Trade' Came to Write its Manifesto." *Resources for Feminist Research* 17: 3.

Calvert, John. (1993). *Pandora's Box: Corporate Power, Free Trade and Canadian Education*. Toronto: Our Schools, Our Selves.

Cameron, Duncan. (1989). "Political Discourse in the Eighties." In Alain Gagnon and Brian Tanguay, eds., *Canadian Parties in Transition: Discourse, Organization and Representation*. Toronto: Nelson.

Campbell, Robert, and Leslie Pal. (1994). *The Real Worlds of Canadian Politics*. Third edition. Peterborough: Broadview Press.

Canada. (1970). *Report of the Royal Commission on the Status of Women*. Hull: Information Canada.

Canada. (1994a). *Budget Speech*. Ottawa: Department of Finance.

Canada. (1994b). *Improving Social Security in Canada: A Discussion Paper*. Hull: Human Resources Development Canada.

Chapman, Jenny. (1993). *Politics, Feminism and the Reformation of Gender*. New York: Routledge.

Chunn, Dorothy. (1995). "Feminism, Law and Public Policy: Politicizing the Personal." In Nancy Mandell and Ann Duffy, eds., *Canadian Families: Diversity, Conflict and Change*. Toronto: Harcourt, Brace and Company.

Clarkson, Stephen. (1994). "Accentuating Continental Integration: From the National Energy Policy to NAFTA." Paper presented at conference on Canada Outside Québec, Robarts Centre for Canadian Studies, York University, April.

Cohen, Majorie Griffin. (1991). *Women and Economic Structure*. Ottawa: Centre for Policy Alternatives.

———. (1992). "The Canadian Women's Movement and its Efforts to Influence the Canadian Economy." In Constance Backhouse and David Flaherty, eds., *Changing Times: The Women's Movement in Canada and the United States*. Montréal: McGill-Queen's University Press.

———. (1993a). "Social Policy and Social Services." In Pierson, et al. *Canadian Women's Issues, Volume 1: Strong Voices*. Toronto: James Lorimer.

———. (1993b). "Economic Restructuring Through Trade: Implications for People." Paper presented at the Shastri Indo-Canadian Seminar on Economic Change and Economic Development, New Delhi, December.

———. (1995). "Democracy and Trade Agreements: Challenges for Disadvantaged Women, Minorities and States." In Robert Boyer and Daniel Drache, eds., *Do Nation-States Have a Future?* Kingston: McGill-Queen's University Press.

Cook, Ramsey, and Wendy Mitchinson, eds. (1976). *The Proper Sphere.* Toronto: Oxford University Press.

Corrigan, Philip, and Derek Sayer. (1985). *The Great Arch: English State Formation as Cultural Revolution.* London: Basil Blackwell.

Cox, Robert. (1991). "The Global Political Economy and Social Choice." In Daniel Drache and Meric Gertler, eds., *The New Era of Global Competition: State Policy and Market Power.* Montréal: McGill-Queen's University Press.

————. (1994). "Global Restructuring: Making Sense of the Changing International Political Economy." In Richard Stubbs and Geoffrey Underhill, eds., *Politcal Economy and the Changing Global Order.* Toronto: McClelland and Stewart.

Day, Shelagh. (1993). "Speaking for Ourselves." In Kenneth McRoberts and Patrick Monaham, eds., *The Charlottetown Accord, the Referendum, and the Future of Canada.* Toronto: University of Toronto Press.

Davis, Mike. (1984). "The Political Economy of Late and Imperial America." *New Left Review* 123.

Deblock, Christian, and Michele Rioux. (1993). "NAFTA: The Trump Card of the United States." *Studies in Political Economy* 41 (Summer).

Drache, Daniel. (1992). "Conclusion." In Daniel Drache, ed., *Getting on Track: Social Democratic Strategies for Ontario.* Kingston: McGill-Queen's University Press.

————. (1994). "The Post-National State." In James Bickerton and Alain Gagnon, eds., *Canadian Politics.* Second Edition. Peterborough: Broadview Press.

————, and Meric Gertler. (1991). "Introduction." In Daniel Drache and Meric Gertler, eds., *The New Era of Global Competition: State Policy and Market Power.* Montréal: McGill-Queen's University Press.

ECE, Regional Preparatory Meeting. (1994). *Wealth of Nations—Poverty of Women.* Vienna, October.

Eisenstein, Zillah. (1988). *The Female Body and the Law.* Los Angeles: University of California Press.

Elson, Dianne. (1992). "From Survival Strategies to Transformation Strategies." In Lourdes Beneria and Shelley Feldman, eds., *Unequal Burden: Economic Crisis, Personal Poverty and Women's Work.* Boulder: Westview Press.

Esping-Anderson, Gosta. (1990). *The Three Worlds of Welfare Capitalism.* Princeton: Princeton University Press.

Evans, Patricia. (1995). "Ontario's Welfare Policy: Restructuring the Debate." In Janine Brodie, ed., *Women and Canadian Public Policy.* Toronto: Harcourt, Brace and Company.

Findlay Sue. (1987). "Facing the State: The Politics of the Women's Movement Reconsidered." In Heather Jon Maroney and Meg Luxton, eds., *Feminism and Political Economy: Women's Work, Women's Struggles*. Toronto: Methuen.

———. (1988). "Feminist Struggles with the Canadian State, 1966-1988." *Resources for Feminist Research* 17: 3 (September).

Fink-Eitel, Hinrich. (1992). *Foucault: An Introduction*. Philadelphia: Pennbridge Books.

Foucault, Michel. (1973). *Madness and Civilization: A History of Insanity in the Age of Reason*. Translated by R. Howard. New York: Random House.

Fox Piven, Frances. (1990). "Ideology and the State: Women, Power and the Welfare State." In Linda Gordon, ed., *Women, the State, and Welfare*. Madison: University of Wisconsin Press.

Fransway, Suzanne, Diane Court, and R.W. Connell. (1989). *Staking a Claim: Feminism, Bureaucracy and the State*. Sydney: Allen and Unwin.

Fraser, Nancy. (1989). *Unruly Practices: Power, Discourse and Gender in Contemporary Social Theory*. Minneapolis: University of Minnesota Press.

———. (1990). "Struggle Over Needs: Outline of a Socialist-Feminist Critical Theory of Late Capitalist Political Culture." In Linda Gordon, ed., *Women, the State, and Welfare*. Madison: University of Wisconsin Press.

———, and Linda Gordon. (1994). "A Geneology of Dependency: Tracing a Keyword of the US Welfare State." *Signs* 19: 2 (Winter).

Friedman, Harriet. (1991). "New Wines, New Bottles: The Regulation of Capital on a World Scale." *Studies in Political Economy* 36 (Autumn).

Fudge, Judy. (1989). "The Privatization of the Costs of Reproduction." *Canadian Journal of Women and the Law* 3.

———. (1993). "NAC for Change: Women's No Transformed Debate." *This Magazine* (January/February).

Gabriel, Christina, and Laura Macdonald. (1993). "Women Organizing Around NAFTA: Prospects for a Feminist Internationality." Paper presented at the Structural Change and Gender Relations in the Era of Globalization Workshop, North-South Institute, Toronto, October.

Gamble, Andrew. (1988). *The Free Economy and the Strong State: The Politics of Thatcherism*. Durham, NC: Duke University Press.

Gill, Stephen. (1992). "The Emerging World Order and European Change." In Ralph Miliband and Leo Panitch, eds., *New World Order? Socialist Register 1992*. London: Merlin.

Gordon, Linda. (1990). "The New Feminist Scholarship on the Welfare State." In Linda Gordon, ed., *Women, the State, and Welfare*. Madison: University of Wisconsin Press.

————. (1991). "On Difference." *Genders* 10 (Spring).

Gotell, Lise. (1993). *The Women's Movement, Equality Rights, and the Charter.* Ph.D. dissertation, York University.

————, and Janine Brodie. (1991). "Women and Parties: More than an Issue of Numbers." In Hugh Thorburn, ed., *Party Politics in Canada.* Sixth Edition. Toronto: Prentice-Hall.

Gottlieb, Amy, ed. (1993). "What About Us? Organizing Inclusivity in the National Action Committee on the Status of Women." In Linda Carty, ed., *And Still We Rise.* Toronto: Women's Press.

Gray, Gratton. (1990). "Social Policy by Stealth." *Policy Options* 11: 2

Greaves, Lorraine. (1991). "Reorganizing the National Action Committee on the Status of Women 1986-1988." In Jeri White and Janice Ristock, eds., *Women and Social Change: Feminist Activism in Canada.* Toronto: James Lorimer.

Grinspun, Ricardo, and Robert Kreklewich. (1994). "Consolidating Neoliberal Reforms: 'Free Trade' as a Conditioning Framework." *Studies in Political Economy* 43 (Spring).

Grosz, Elizabeth. (1990). "Conclusion: A Note on Essentialism and Difference." In Sneja Gunew, ed., *Feminist Knowledge: Critique and Construct.* New York: Routledge.

Gunew, Sneja, and Anna Yeatman, eds. (1993). *Feminism and the Politics of Difference.* Halifax: Fernwood Publishing.

Haraway, Donna. (1991). *Simians, Cyborgs and Women: The Reinvention of Nature.* New York: Routledge.

Harvey, David. (1989). *The Condition of Postmodernity.* London: Basil Blackwell.

Held, David. et al., eds. (1983). *States and Societies.* Oxford: Open University Press.

Hernes, Helga. (1987). *Welfare State and Women Power: Essays in State Formation.* Oslo: Norwegian University Press.

Jameson, Fredric. (1993). "Postmodernism, or the Cultural Logic of Late Capitalism." In Thomas Dogherty, ed., *Postmodernism: A Reader.* New York: Columbia University Press.

Jenson, Jane. (1990a). "Wearing Your Adjectives Proudly: Citizenship and Gender in Turn-of-the-Century Canada." Paper presented at the Annual Meeting of the Canadian Political Science Association, Victoria, British Columbia.

————. (1990b). "Representations in Crisis: The Roots of Canada's Permeable Fordism." *Canadian Journal of Political Science* 23: 4 (December).

————. (1991a). "All the World's a Stage: Ideas, Spaces and Times in Canadian Political Economy." *Studies in Political Economy* 36 (Fall).

————. (1991b). "Citizenship and Equity: Variations Across Time and

Space." Royal Commission on Electoral Reform and Party Financing, Vol. 12 *Political Ethics: A Canadian Perspective*. Toronto: Dundurn Press.

Jessop, Bob. (1990). "Regulation Theories in Retrospect and Prospect." *Economy and Society* 19: 2 (May).

———. (1993). "Toward a Schumpeterian Workfare State? Preliminary Remarks on Post-Fordist Political Economy." *Studies in Political Economy* 40 (Spring).

Jones, Kathleen. (1990). "Citizenship in a Woman-Friendly Polity." *Signs* 15: 4 (Summer).

———. (1993). *Compassionate Authority*. New York: Routledge.

Khosla, Punam. (1993). "Review of the Situation of Women in Canada." Toronto: National Action Committee on the Status of Women.

Kome, Penny. (1993). "The Turning Point: NAC and the Referendum." *Newest Review* (February/March).

Krugman, Paul. (1994). "Competition: A Dangerous Obsession." *Foreign Affairs* 73: 2 (March).

Lamoureux, Diane. (1987). "Nationalism and Feminism in Québec: An Impossible Attraction." In Heather Jon Maroney and Meg Luxton, eds., *Feminism and Political Economy*. Toronto: Methuen.

Larner, Wendy. (1993). "Changing Contexts: Globalization, Migration and Feminism in New Zealand." In Sneja Gunew and Anna Yeatman, eds., *Feminism and the Politics of Difference*. Halifax: Fernwood Publishing.

Laycock, David. (1994). "Reforming Canadian Democracy? Institutions and Ideology in the Reform Party Project." *Canadian Journal of Political Science* 27: 2.

Leger, Huguette, and Judy Rebick. (1993), *The NAC Voters' Guide*. Hull: National Action Committee on the Status of Women.

Lipietz, Alain. (1987). *Mirages and Miracles*. London: Verso Books.

Macdonell, Diane. (1986). *Theories of Discourse: An Introduction*. New York: Basil Blackwell.

MacKinnon, Catherine. (1989). *Towards a Feminist Theory of the State*. Cambridge: Harvard University Press.

Magnussen, Warren, and Rob Walker. (1988). "De-centring the State: Political Theory and Canadian Political Economy." *Studies in Political Economy* 26 (Summer).

Manning, Preston. (1992). *The New Canada*. Toronto: Macmillan.

Maroney, Heather Jon, and Meg Luxton, eds. 1987. *Feminism and Political Economy: Women's Work, Women's Struggles*. Toronto: Methuen.

Marshall, T.H. (1977). *Class, Citizenship, and Social Democracy*. Chicago: University of Chicago Press.

McBride, Stephen, and John Shields. (1993). *Dismantling a Nation: Canada and the New World Order*. Halifax: Fernwood Publishing.

McDaniel, Susan. (1993). "Where the Contradictions Meet: Women and Family Security in Canada in the 1990s." In National Forum on Family Security. *Family Securities in Insecure Times*. Ottawa: Canadian Council on Social Development.

McDowell, Linda. (1991). "Life Without Father and Ford: The New Gender Order of Post-Fordism." *Transnational Institute of British Geography* 16: 400-19.

McDowell, Linda, and Rosemary Pringle, eds. (1992). *Defining Women: Social Institutions and Gender Divisions*. London: Polity Press.

McFarland, Joan. (1993). "Combining Economic and Social Policy Through Work and Welfare: The Impact on Women." Paper presented to the Economic Equity Workshop, Status of Women, Ottawa.

McIntosh, Mary. (1978). "The State and the Oppression of Women." In Annette Kuhn and Ann Marie Wolpe, eds., *Feminism and Materialism*. London: Routledge and Kegan Paul.

McNay, Lois. (1992). *Foucault and Feminism*. Boston: Northeastern University Press.

McQuaig, Linda. (1992). "The Fraying of Our Social Safety Net." *The Toronto Star* (8 November).

Mouffe, Chantal. (1993). *The Return of the Political*. London: Verso Books.

National Action Committee on the Status of Women. (1992). "Review of the Situation of Women in Canada—1992." Toronto: NAC.

National Forum on Family Security. (1993). *Family Security in Insecure Times*. Ottawa: Canadian Council on Social Development.

National Women's Consultation on the Social Security Review. (1994). Ottawa.

Nicholson, Linda. (1992). "Feminist Theory: The Private and the Public." In Linda McDowell and Rosemary Pringle, eds., *Defining Women: Social Institutions and Gender Divisions*. London: Polity Press.

Okin, Susan Moller. (1979). *Women in Western Political Thought*. Princeton, NJ: Princeton University Press.

Ontario. (1987). *The Free Trade Agreement and Women*. Toronto: Ontario Women's Directorate.

———. (1993). *The North American Free Trade Agreement: Implications for Women*. Toronto: Ontario Women's Directorate.

Orloff, Ann Shola. (1993). "Gender and the Social Rights of Citizenship: The Comparative Analysis of Gender Relations and Welfare States." *American Sociological Review* 58 (June).

Pal, Leslie. (1993). *Interests of the State: The Politics of Language, Multiculturalism and Feminism in Canada*. Montréal: McGill-Queen's University Press.

Panitch, Leo. (1993). "Globalization, States and the Left: Nafta Through the Looking Glass." Paper presented to El Mundo Actual: Situacion y Alternatives. Mexico City, December.

Pateman, Carole. (1988). *The Sexual Contract*. Stanford: Stanford University Press.

———. (1989). *The Disorder of Women*. London: Polity Press.

———. (1992). "The Patriarchal Welfare State." In Linda McDowell and Rosemary Pringle, eds., *Defining Women: Social Institutions and Gender Divisions*. London: Polity Press.

Patten, Steve. (1994). "A Political Economy of Reform: Understanding Middle-Class Support for Manning's Right-Libertarian Populism." Paper presented at the Annual Meeting of the Canadian Political Science Association, Calgary.

Phillips, Anne. (1991). *Engendering Democracy*. Pittsburgh: Pennsylvania State University Press.

Phillips, Susan. (1991). *Projects, Pressure and Perceptions of Effectiveness: An Organizational Analysis of National Canadian Women's Groups*. Unpublished Ph.D. Thesis, Carleton University, Ottawa.

———. (1992). "How Ottawa Blends: Shifting Government Relationships with Interest Groups." In Francine Abele, ed., *How Ottawa Spends 1992-93: A More Democratic Canada?* Ottawa: Carleton University Press.

Pierson, Ruth Roach. (1993). "The Mainstream Women's Movement and the Politics of Difference." In Ruth Roach Pierson, Majorie Griffin Cohen, Paula Bourne, and Philinda Masters. *Canadian Women's Issues, Volume 1: Strong Voices*. Toronto: James Lorimer.

Pringle, Rosemary, and Sophie Watson. (1990). "Fathers, Brothers, and Mates: The Fraternal State in Australia." In Sophie Watson, ed., *Playing the State: Australian Feminist Interventions*. London: Verso Books.

———. (1992). "Women's Interests and the Post-Structuralist State." In Michele Barrett and Anne Phillips, eds., *Destabilizing Theory: Contemporary Feminist Debates*. Stanford: Stanford University Press.

Randall, Melanie. (1988). "Feminism and the State: Questions for Theory and Practice." *Resources for Feminist Research* 17: 3 (September).

Rebick, Judy. (1993). "The Charlottetown Accord: A Faulty Framework and a Wrong Headed Compromise." In Kenneth McRoberts and Patrick Monahan, eds., *The Charlottetwon Accord, the Referendum, and the Future of Canada*. Toronto: University of Toronto Press.

———. (1994). "Interview with Judy Rebick." *Studies in Political Economy* 44 (September).

Rice, James, and Michael Prince. (1993). "Lowering the Safety Net and Weaking the Bonds of Nationhood: Social Policy in Mulroney Years."

In Susan Phillips, ed.. *How Ottawa Spends, 1992-93: A More Democratic Canada?* Ottawa: Carleton University Press.

Robinson, Ian. (1993a). *North American Trade As If Democracy Mattered.* Ottawa: Canadian Centre For Policy Alternatives.

————. (1993b). "The NAFTA, Democracy and Continental Integration." In Susan Phillips, ed., *How Ottawa Spends, 1992-93: A More Democratic Canada?* Ottawa: Carleton University Press.

Sapiro, Virginia. (1990). "The Gender Basis of American Social Policy." In Linda Gordon, ed., *Women, the State, and Welfare.* Madison: University of Wisconsin Press.

Schreader, Alicia. (1990). "The State-Funded Women's Movement: A Case of Two Political Agendas." In Roxanna Ng, Gillian Walker and Jacob Muller, eds., *Community Organization and the Canadian State.* Toronto: Garamond Press.

Sigurdson, Richard. (1994). "Preston Manning and the Politics of Postmodernism in Canada." *Canadian Journal of Political Science* 27.

Siim, Birte. (1988). "Toward a Feminist Rethinking of the Welfare State." In Kathleen Jones and Anna Jonasdottir, eds., *The Political Interests of Gender.* Newbury Park, CA: Sage Publications.

Siltanen, J., and M. Stanworth. (1984). *Women in the Public Sphere: A Critique of Sociology and Politics.* London: Hutchinson Co. Ltd.

Soja, Edward. (1989). *Postmodern Geographies.* London: Verso Books.

Spears, John. (1993). "Wells Tries New Spin on Welfare." *The Toronto Star* 18 December, A4.

Stubbs, Richard, and Geoffrey Underhill, eds. (1994). *Political Economy and the Changing Global Order.* Toronto: McClelland and Stewart.

Trofimenkoff, Susan Mann. (1983). *The Dream of a Nation.* Toronto: Gage.

Underhill, Geoffrey. (1994). "Conceptualizing the Changing Global Order." In Richard Stubbs and Geoffrey Underhill, eds., *Political Economy and the Changing Global Order.* Toronto: McClelland and Stewart.

Ursel, Jane. (1992). *Private Lives, Public Policy: 100 Years of State Intervention in the Family.* Toronto: Women's Press.

US Agency for International Development. (1992). "Gender and Adjustment." Washington: USAID.

Valpy, Michael. (1993). "The Myth of the Myth of Canadian Compassion." In National Forum on Family Security. *Family Security in Insecure Times.* Ottawa: Canadian Council on Social Development.

Valverde, Mariana. (1992). "When the Mother of the Race is Free: Race, Reproduction and Sexuality in First-Wave Feminism." In Franca Iacovetta and Mariana Valverde, eds., *Gender Conflicts: New Essays in Women's History.* Toronto: University of Toronto Press.

Vickers, Jill. (1991). "Bending the Iron Law of the Oligarchy." In Jeri Dawn

Wine and Janice Ristock, eds., *Women and Social Change: Feminist Activism in Canada*. Toronto: James Lorimer.

―――. (1992). "The Intellectual Origins of the Women's Movements in Canada." In Constance Backhouse and David Flaherty, eds., *Changing Times: The Women's Movement in Canada and the United States*. Montréal: McGill-Queen's University Press.

―――, Pauline Rankin, and Christine Appelle. (1993). *Politics as if Women Mattered*. Toronto: University of Toronto Press.

Walzer, Michael. (1984). "Liberalism and the Art of Separation." *Political Theory* 12 (August).

Watson, Sophie. (1990). "The State of Play: An Introduction." In Sophie Watson, ed., *Playing the State: Australian Feminist Interventions*. London: Verso Books.

Williams, Fiona. (1989). *Social Policy: A Critical Introduction*. London: Polity Press.

Williams, Toni. (1990). "Re-forming 'Women's' Truth: A Critique of the Report of the Royal Commission on the Status of Women in Canada." *Ottawa Law Review* 22: 3.

Wilson, Elizabeth. (1977). *Women and the Welfare State*. London: Tavistock.

―――. (1988). *Hallucinations: Life in the Postmodern City*. London: Radius.

Wine, Jeri Dawn, and Janice Ristock, eds. *Women and Social Change: Feminist Activism in Canada*. Toronto: Lorimer.

Woman to Woman. (1993). *Changing Economies: Free Trade and the Global Agenda*. Toronto: Global Strategies.

Yeatman, Anna. (1984). "Despotism and Civil Society: The Limits of Patriarchal Citizenship." In J.H. Stiehm. ed., *Women's View of the Political World of Men*. Dobbs Ferry, NY: Transnational Publishers.

―――. (1990). *Bureaucrats, Technocrats, Femocrats: Essays on the Contemporary Australian State*. Sydney: Allen and Unwin.

―――. (1993). "Voice and Representation in the Politics of Difference." In Sneja Gunew and Anna Yeatman, eds., *Feminism and the Politics of Difference*. Halifax: Fernwood Publishing.

―――. (1994). *Postmodern Revisionings of the Political*. New York: Routledge.

York, Geoffrey. (1993). "Social Programs Called Outdated." *The Globe and Mail* 17 November, AI.

Young, Iris Marion. (1989). "Polity and Group Difference: A Critique of Universal Citizenship. *Ethics* 99.

―――. (1990). *Throwing Like A Girl and Other Essays in Feminist Philosophy and Social Theory*. Bloomington: Indiana University Press.